The Turn to Applied Ethics:
Practical Consequences for Research, Education,
and the Role of Ethicists in Public Debate

The Turn to Applied Ethics:
Practical Consequences
for Research, Education, and
the Role of Ethicists in Public Debate

Societas Ethica

Proceedings of the 1992 Conference of the European Society for Research in Ethics (Societas Ethica)

Woudschoten/Utrecht 24-28 August 1992

F.R. Heeger & T. van Willigenburg (eds.)

Kok Pharos Publishing House – Kampen

CIP-GEGEVENS KONINKLIJKE BIBLIOTHEEK, DEN HAAG

© 1993, Kok Pharos Publishing House,
P.O. Box 5019, 8260 AG Kampen, the Netherlands
Cover Design By Rob Lucas
ISBN 90 390 0048 4
NUGI 611/635

Preface

In recent years ethics has entered the field of social discussion and political decision-making on various kinds of moral issues. Ethicists are assigned a role as consultant on the moral dimensions of policies, decisions and actions. Ethicists are, for instance, asked to serve on ethics-committees in hospitals, or to act as in-house experts with large firms, in order to provide for advice on moral questions of management and business.

As a result of this appeal there has been a rapid development of several specializations in the field of applied ethics, like bio-ethics, environmental ethics, and business ethics.

This turn to applied ethics has some very important consequences for the academic work of moral philosophers and moral theologians. These consequences concern the aim and content of academic ethical *research*, as well as the aim and content of academic *teaching* in ethics. But the turn to applied ethics also demands serious reflection on the *role of ethicists in public debate*.

Thorough reflection on the consequences of the turn to applied ethics was the theme and aim of the 1992 yearly conference of the Societas Ethica – the European Society for Research in Ethics – which was held in Woudschoten/Utrecht, the Netherlands. Next to the presentation of recent research, the conference aimed at a comparison and evaluation of the experiences of moral philosophers and moral theologians coming from the 19 countries which are represented in the Societas Ethica.

This volume collects four lectures and one paper which were presented during the conference, covering the main themes (research, education and public role), and posing many of the crucial questions, together with some answers which are alternately tentative, well-founded, and provocative.

We hope that this volume not only contributes to the reflection of ethicists about their work and efforts, but also shows how fruitfull a conference may be which brings together scholars from very different locations and traditions.

Utrecht, May 1993
the editors

Contents

What is Meant by 'The Turn to Applied Ethics'?

Robert Heeger

Is there reason to speak of a 'turn'?

There is at present a certain societal demand for ethical advice. Government bodies, business enterprises or research institutes are asking ethicists for some assistance. The reason is often that there are decisions to be made which also have moral import and that those who have to take the decisions think it useful to consider these decisions in company with some who are competent in the field of ethics. Quite a few ethicists are ready to accept such invitations. They are members of a public advisory board, a hospital ethics committee or an animal experiment committee, or they are working as ethics consultants for the management of a firm. Problems typical of this advisory activity are increasingly treated also in academic departments of ethics or moral theology. There have even emerged various specializations, such as bio-ethics, environmental ethics, management-ethics or marked-ethics.

This situation took shape in the course of the last two decades. Is it justified to call its emergence 'the turn to applied ethics'? There are reasons to doubt this. Does such a claim not presuppose that all previous ethics was abstract, and is this judgement not wrong? An adequately pursued ethics has always been occupied with human action. In dealing with the good and meaningful life it has been focussed on the improvement of human action. It has had a practical interest. Therefore, in the classical ethical texts there is, beside the unfolded theory, always a discussion of practical cases. Think, e. g., of Aristotle, Thomas, Hobbes or Hume. Against this background the expression 'applied ethics' seems downright pleonastic.

However, one might speak of a 'turn' in a much more modest way. One might not presuppose that all previous ethics was abstract, but only hold that modern ethics was abstract. One might, e. g., put forward that academic moral philosophy in German-speaking countries, untill this century under the influence of Kantianism, concentrated upon so-called questions of principle and took rather little interest in applied ethics. One might also maintain that academic moral philosophy in the English-speaking world, impressed by logical positivism, divided the world into logic, facts and values, entrusted the facts to the special branches of science, dismissed the values as a matter of emotion, fell back upon the logical analysis of moral language and left concrete ethics out of consideration. But are these examples of wellknown 'schools' sufficient for the judgement that modern ethics was abstract? Was there not also special ethics, directed to deliminated practical subjects? Many of those who taught us ethics dealt with special ethics as well. Thus, why to speak of a 'turn'?

In attempting to answer this question one should specify that which is rather new in the ethics of the last two decades. Perhaps one is correct in saying that this is the combination of four traits.

10

(1) Ethics tries to respond to a growing constraint to which society is exposed: the constraint to make moral decisions. It deals with problems caused, e. g., by the progress of science and technology or by the new difference between the poor and the rich. These problems are posed 'by life itself', that is to say, they are important also for extra-theoretical reasons, they are not invented to illustrate an ethical theory.

(2) Ethics analyses the moral features of these problems and tries to make its concepts and theories fruitful for solving them.

(3) In doing this ethics goes thoroughly into empirical questions, because it can only contribute to satisfactory solutions if it is pursued with sufficient knowledge of the respective field. Specializations, such as bio-ethics, business-ethics etc., bear witness of this. They are necessary because of the complexity of the tasks.

(4) Ethics places its theories in interaction with the context of their application. It does not simply apply its theories but permits that questions of application react upon the theories and that the theories thereby be adjusted. To take one example: Modern ethics widely confined itself to interpersonal relations. This fundamental 'anthropomorphist' idea was revised by many because it proved practically untenable that nobody should be held morally responsible for the destruction of nature.

If the abovementioned combination of four traits really is rather new, then one can speak of a 'turn' without being unfair to classical ethics or modern special ethics. But why is this a question of interest, after all? The answer seems to be that one is asking this question because one tries to make up one's mind how to respond to the turn to applied ethics: Should one approve of this development, or should one rather exercise restraint since applied ethics abandons things which are essential to ethics? To come to grips with this problem one should consider two moot points concerning applied ethics: the role of the ethicist and the role of moral rules and principles.

Coming up to social expectations?

Is the 'turn to applied ethics' a matter of adjusting to new social circumstances? Is it, e. g., that the ethicist has to convert to a behaviour in line with real market conditions and that he has to take a new role? Ethicists have time and again been warned against entering into a dependent relation that threatens their academic integrity.

It is fairly easy to tell which roles an ethicist should not take, even though he may at times be urged to take them. An ethicist should not be a moral guru, that is to say, he should not appear as a moral authority, as one who knows everything about good and evil. Neither should he be a moral ombudsman, a moral reference book, a moral advocate or one who renders everything into a moral problem. He should not be a moral yes-man who only places a moral quality seal on others' policy decisions. He should not pose as a moral educator who aims at attitudinal changes of insensitive rulers or acts as a motivation-manager, and, finally, he should not be a moral prophet or crusader of truth who brands abuses.

One can even give a reason why an ethicist should

avoid these roles: They are incompatible with his specific task. This task consists in doing applied ethics, and doing applied ethics amounts to facilitating decision-making in moral questions. But thereby one has not yet made the point at issue disappear. The ethicist may be wholly devoted to his specific task and yet be in trouble because of social expectations. Take the case of the analytical expertise of the ethicist not contributing to the expected 'solution' of moral problems, but, on the contrary, to the generation of problems, to an elaboration of the problematic nature of certain ways of acting or even of institutions? Think, e. g., of ethical analyses of so-called industrialized stockfarming, of biotechnology or the trans-genesis of cattle. Suppose that, in his analyses, the ethicist has reason to apply a moral principle that prescribes respect for the integrity of animals. Suppose this principle leads the ethicist to a fundamental criticism of the practice. How much resistance from his side, then, is compatible with the facilitating of decision-making that is expected from him?

Abandoning rules and principles?

This issue concerns the 'kernel' of ethics as we know it. Does the 'turn to applied ethics' mean that the work of the ethicist should not any longer be guided by moral rules and principles? Is the ethicist urged to confine himself to situation-specific and local solutions of moral problems? Some maintain this in an impressive way, and some consider it preformed in the Aristotelian theory of practical wisdom.

One of these movements could be called 'community and society'. It claims that moral debates in society are

13

endless. They both go on and on and fail to come to a final result, the reason being that, obviously, in society there is no reasonable way to reach a moral consensus. A notorious example of this is the impossibility of a consensus about abortion. Therefore, applied ethics should abandon the traditional claims of universal validity. It should, instead, focus on community, consider the local practice and, within this framework, try to accomplish an appropriate weighing of means and ways to a good and happy life.

Another movement, indebted to hermeneutical philosophy, stresses the 'productive element of the application of norms'. It maintains that concrete moral problems cannot be solved by simple subsumption under principles. The reason is that principles are general, that cases are individual and concrete, and that the general cannot simply be applied to the concrete, because the standard of the general is codetermined, supplemented and amended by the assessment of the concrete cases.

A third movement champions case-bound reasoning. Its criticism of traditional ethics reads briefly: 'abstraction and unfruitfulness of moral principles'. Proponents of a case-bound reasoning emphasize the following: If one prefers to discuss moral issues, such as the question of abortion, on the level of abstract theories and general principles, then one can be almost certain, that on the practical level this discussion will reach an impasse. Therefore, applied ethics avoids 'questions of principle'. It concentrates on finding satisfactory solutions in individual cases. A morally satisfactory solution does not need any abstract principles. What it needs is a spe-

14

cific sensitivity for the singular case and practical wisdom related to the context of this case, that is to say, a capacity to consider carefully the different dimensions of the case.

Does applied ethics really call for such a radical reorientation? One may affirm that there is a 'productive element of the application of norms' and that many moral problems cannot be solved by simple subsumption, following the pattern 'principle-inference-conclusion'. But this does not commit one to do without moral rules or principles. Is it actually possible to do without them, and is it on the whole possible to confine oneself to situation-specific and local solutions of moral problems? These questions can be answered in the negative and reasons can be given. It may be granted that applied ethics, surely, has to analyze and evaluate individual cases, but it can at the same time be maintained that there is more to applied ethics. Surely, even context-related decisions of practical wisdom should be comprehensible and possible to duplicate, that is to say, even they should be decisions on the basis of reasons. But if for decisions reasons are to be given, then inevitably also general points of view underlie them.

Moreover, one can ask what actually sets moral considerations of concrete cases going. That actions or situations are of a morally problematic nature is, surely, not something which clinges to them 'in themselves'. They acquire their morally problematic nature only in a moral perspective. But is to have a moral perspective solely to have a specific sensitivity for a concrete individual case or intuitively to interpret a state of affairs as a moral case? Doesn't a moral perspective also comprise that one has general moral beliefs such as those expressed in rules or principles?

Finally, one can put forward something important about the matter of applied ethics. It is not only individual actions in specific situations that applied ethics deals with. Applied ethics is also occupied with general ways of acting, with political, institutionalized, public practice. But in this activity its object of reflection is not the individual case, but the 'normal case'. Decisions have to be made whether a general way of acting is admissible or inadmissible, e. g., whether or not it is morally right to expose animals to genetic manipulation in order to improve productivity or to raise resistance to disease. But if one wants to make decisions on principle one must use arguments on principle and go into discussions about principles.

Concluding: What is meant by 'the turn to applied ethics'? In a first approximation one can answer this question by simply pointing to a combination of traits that is rather new in ethics. But as soon as one considers some moot points, e. g. te role of the ethicist or that of moral rules and principles, the answer is still open. Those who are doing applied ethics will have to give the answer themselves, because they have to make up their minds about the moot points.

About the author:
prof. dr. F.R. Heeger is full professor of Ethics at the Utrecht University – The Netherlands (Department of Philosophy and Department of Theology)

16

The Turn to Applied Ethics

Practical Consequences for Research

Introduction

The turn to applied ethics raises the question about the contribution of ethical research to answering practical moral quandaries. What is the nature of research in *applied* ethics? How does it relate to the academic work which moral philosophers and moral theologians have been doing without being challanged by practical questions in the first place? What is the task and role of the 'applied' ethicist as scholar?

In the first article of this section, Frans Jacobs sketches the possibilities ánd the limits of the contribution of ethical research to the solution of practical problems. Ethicists have a paradoxical task, he says. On the one hand they have to bring closer the problems under consideration. In so far as they have a certain familiarity with analogous problem cases, they can, by exposing the differences and the similarities with these other cases, slightly reduce the strangeness of the case under consideration and, in doing so, make preparations for a responsible decision. On the other hand, ethicists have to augment the distance between ourselves and the problems with which we are confronted. They can do so by paying attention to the frameworks within which we are used to look at practical problems, and about which we hardly ever think, just because they are so familiar.

Jan Vorstenbosch, in the second article, elaborates this picture of nearness and distance by distinguishing four possible purposes and objects of research in applied ethics. The Sophistic approach stresses the contribution of ethical research to the improvement of the rationality of public debate and practical decision-making. The Socratic approach takes more distance. It does not help practitioners by construing better arguments, but irritates them by questioning opinions, reasons and justifications, thus trying to lay bare the ideological structures and established presuppositions which underly the moral questions posed. The Platonic approach stresses the need to develop a substantial (and true) ethical theory which may be applied, in a more or less deductive way, to practical problems. The Aristotelian approach brings the moral philosopher or moral theologian again close to the actual moral experiences, attitudes, manners and moral reactions of people in a particular culture or context. According to this approach ethical research should try to interpret these experiences and the ethos on which they are based. Applied ethics should be hermeneutics of moral experience.

After distinguishing various types of research in applied ethics, there is always a tendency to plea for a combination of all these approaches in one 'ideal' research programm. Ethical research should creatively play the game of nearness and distance. Still, there is need of more reflection on the strong and weak points of the proposed types of research. Only further meta-reflection on the possiblities and limitations of different approaches will make research in applied ethics really a winning game.

Concrete Ethics
as a Play of Closeness and Distance[1]

Frans Jacobs

This article is about concrete or applied ethics. The first question then is what expression could be used best: 'concrete ethics' or 'applied ethics'? Sticking to the expression 'concrete ethics' I could start with a short text of Hegel, headed 'Who thinks in abstractions?'.[2] There Hegel puts on the scene a man who is under sentence of death and who is led to the place of execution. The common folk see the man as a murderer and as nothing else. A few ladies call him sturdily built, beautiful and interesting. A priest, 'who knows the bottom of things and the hearts', adds to this that it shows depravity to call a murderer beautiful. All these people are of the opinion that they say something determinate and concrete when they call someone a murderer, beautiful or depraved; but according to Hegel they think completely abstract. Thinking concrete is the person who, for example, investigates what kind of education the criminal has had, what went wrong with it, and who maybe discovers that the criminal once committed a small transgression to which the authorities reacted with unduly harshness, which caused embitterment in this person against the rule of law, etc. So concrete knowledge expresses the essence of the deed and the culprit. Philosophical knowledge in this sense is more concrete than knowledge people usually have; what Hegel calls the speculative concept is then the most concrete kind of knowledge.

Affiliating oneself in the beginning of a paper with a text from Hegel is, of course, splendid, and will surely give the impression of a philosophical depth which I do not possess. Let us, therefore, be satisfied with the expression 'applied ethics'.

What about applied ethics? What is the paradigm of knowledge that can be applied? We find this knowledge primarily in the execution of *techne*, in the process of making things.[3] A craftsman disposes beforehand of a plan or blueprint and he knows exactly the rules of execution for this plan. If the execution goes according to plan, there is no possibility of surprise: the means adjust themselves to the purposive activity. Of course, frequently the tool is found to be damaged and the material not suited. That gives the tool a 'unreadiness-to-hand'[4], as Heidegger calls it. In these circumstances the craftsman has to abandon the execution of his plan in the originally conceived sense. This implies by no means that the adjusted plan is more perfect than the original plan. The application does not add to the *techne* anything essential that was not considered before. The means are improved in order to accomplish better the beforehand completely determined goal.

These characteristics of *techne* are absent in ethics. Applied ethics is different from applied technics in at least two respects. First, what is morally obligatory cannot be determined independently from the concrete circumstances of the case in question. There doesn't exist a moral code of law in which a person can look up what to do if he sees a child drowning before his eyes.

22

According to the Dutch Penal Code, a book that doesn't impress one as immoral, one must come to the rescue of someone who is in immediate danger of life, 'when one cannot dread reasonably a danger for one-self or for others' (§ 450). What, however, does 'reasonably' mean? That is left undecided. Jurisprudence has to decide in matters of law and so expands the law in interpreting it. In matters of ethics we are driven back to what Aristotle calls *phronesis*, the virtue of practical insight. This shows that what is morally obligatory cannot be settled independently from the concrete circumstances of the case in point; the moral significance of a case cannot be determined independently from these circumstances.

That was the first distinction between applied ethics and applied technics. The second distinction is connected with the first: in ethics, unlike in the case of technics, one cannot determine the goal independently from the means. For the means are not morally neutral: whoever would want to bring closer a moral goal by immoral means would remove by this very act the moral element in his goal. In moral issues there is an internal relation between means and ends: someone, for example, who sacrifices human beings in the hope of improving human existence, would show by this action that human existence doesn't matter very much to him. In moral issues the selected means bear witness to the meaning of the goal pursued. That was the second distinction between applied ethics and applied technics.

All this can be summarized as follows: in the case of technics application does not add anything essential to the preceding knowledge, but in the case of ethics it is the application that gives knowledge its full import. Indeed Aristotle said something like this when he wrote:

> "Because the end aimed at is not knowledge but action."[5]

Why, then, do so many representatives of philosophical ethics entertain a suspicion of applied ethics? Maybe they conceive of applied ethics as modelled after applied technics. In that case application is indeed detrimental to a fundamental ethics. But that model is fundamentally misplaced.

It would be better, perhaps, to model applied ethics on hermeneutics. There, too, one speaks of application, and Gadamer has shown in *Wahrheit und Methode (Truth and Method)* that application is not something that occurs when all work is done, not something that is really superfluous, but that during the process of understanding an application occurs out of the text that is to be interpreted to the situation of the interpreter. Without a question beforehand derived from our own 'horizon of understanding' a text would remain closed and strange to us. Dealing with the text leads in turn to a revision of the original question, which in its turn makes possible a renewed understanding of the text: so we move on in an infinite propulsion inside the hermeneutic circle. This is interpreted by Gadamer as the application of something general to something specific: the general element consists in the tradition, understood differently in different periods; what is understood in a specific period is derived from the concrete and specific situation of the interpreter (p.295).

Linking up with this model one could call philosophical ethics a hermeneutics of moral experience, which only reveals its full meaning in its application.[6] One could even call moral experience itself hermeneutical: it makes explicit in every new situation what is to count as courage, loyalty, or a regard for human beings as ends in themselves. So an increasing number of people have the conviction that it is compatible with the regard for human life as an end in itself to bring about euthanasia in case of incurable and painful disease, provided the patient fosters the serious, explicit and prolonged desire to have his life terminated. According to Kant such a regard is, of course, *not* compatible with suicide and euthanasia. The possibility of deriving voluntary euthanasia from the regard for human life as an end in itself is obviously not a matter of mechanical application of an already completed principle, but rather a productive continuation of a principle that reveals its implications only in its application.

Without having read Gadamer, many of the adherents of applied ethics have correctly interpreted their business, nevertheless. This is clearly visible in the work of the adherents of 'reflective equilibrium', a method going back to Rawls. This is not, as is well known, a purely inductive process: it doesn't simply generalize experiences. Nor is it purely deductive: it doesn't design principles independent from experience. In the method of reflective equilibrium mutually inconsistent intuitions on the one hand and principles on the other are confronted with each other in successive cycles, until a state of equilibrium emerges – at least a provisional equilibrium. So the original intuitions and principles are subjected to a learning process in which the application of principles to concrete cases clarifies their real meaning. What Rawls calls 'reflective equilibrium' can be compared with Gadamer's 'fusion of horizons', in which the strangeness of the historical horizon and the familiarity of the present horizon are blended in a supervised way. In the same manner deliberate judgments and traditional ethical theories and principles are united with each other in the work of Rawls.

The strangeness of the historical horizon and the familiarity of the present horizon are blended in a supervised way, I said. There is a play here of closeness and distance. According to Gadamer the true place of hermeneutics is the intervening space between strangeness and familiarity:

> "The place between strangeness and familiarity that the tradition has for us, is between the historically meant factuality and the belonging to a tradition."
> (p. 279.)

In an analogous way one can call reflective equilibrium an intervening space between closeness and distance. This is clearly visible in the twist our colleague Theo van Willigenburg has given to the method of Rawls.[7] He develops a 'case-oriented approach to moral reasoning', in which he confronts a new, problematical case with clear and familiar cases. Our concern with familiar cases serves as a fixed point from where we diminish the distance that separates us from new cases:

> "Thus, in general, the growing expertise of the ethical practioner will be reflected by a gradual movement on the scale from 'new and unfamiliar problems' to 'clear and familiar problems'." (p. 140)

That doesn't mean that the new always has to be adapted to the old. It is also possible that a new case is an inducement to dissociate ourselves from a way of acting that we were accustomed to, and that we adopt a new way of acting. For one can imagine that not the new is strange to us, but rather the old. In this sense Hegel wrote:

> "What is familiar is not known simply because it is familiar. It is the most common self-deception and deception of others to presuppose something as familiar when it comes to knowledge, and to accept this; but with all its talking back and forth such knowledge without knowing what is happening to it, never gets anywhere."[8]

Because none of its elements (intuitions and principles) is excluded from criticism or revision, reflective equilibrium, the result of the movement caused by criticism and revision, resembles the transparent and simple state of rest in which according to Hegel the dialectical movement ends:

> "The true is thus the bacchanalian whirl in which no member is not drunken; and because each, as soon as it detaches itself, dissolves immediately – the whirl is just as much transparent and simple repose." (p. 39)

If I equate, however, reflective equilibrium with Gadamer's fusing of horizons and this in turn with Hegel's bacchanalian whirl, then there is a threat that the play of closeness and distance will end up in the abolition of all distinctions. Then we find ourselves in the night in which according to Hegel all cows are black (p. 19). Clearly there is a distinction between Hegel's dialectic and Gadamer's fusion of horizons. As is well known, Hegelian dialectic knows at the end of its movement nothing strange outside itself anymore; Gadamer on the other hand is of the opinion that the unremovable finiteness of man makes it impossible for experience ever to close. With this point an adherent of reflective equilibrium would agree. He would, however, disagree with Gadamer in not sharing his conservative prejudices concerning the 'classical'. Gadamer expresses this as follows:

"Classical is, what stands up against historical criticism, because the authority of its history, the compelling force of its ongoing and self-assured validity, already precedes all historical reflection and perseveres in it." (p. 271)

But according to the adherent of reflective equilibrium nothing in principle can stand firm against the criticism of history.

'Nothing can stand firm against the criticism of history': that sounds heroic. One can question whether the adherent of reflective equilibrium can maintain his critical pose. What does he answer to the simple question of whether his method in the final analysis can do more than give a coherent ordering of his own prejudices? For his method is not absolutist, but appeals to coherence: it reconciles intuitions, information, principles and traditional theories with one another. Listen to Van Willigenburg:

28

"Given our shared (moral) nature and our experiences as participants in a common tradition there is reason to expect that there will be some agreement on intuitive moral insights."[9]

Such intuitive moral insights have a truly classical status in Gadamer's sense; they are above criticism. What, however, if certain intuitive moral insights that we all share would, due to an unexpected turn of events, be illuminated in the true light of their historical contingency and arbitrariness? The play between closeness and distance would reach a higher level and we would perhaps, confronted with a crack in our common tradition, have to make a break with our old moral insights. In this connection I would like to refer briefly to the work of Hans Jonas. He writes that

"... before our time man's inroads into nature, as seen by himself, were essentially superficial and powerless to upset its appointed balance."[10]

This situation has changed dramatically, and this in turn has brought to light some 'characteristics of previous ethics' from which we should distance ourselves now. Sketching the history of ethics till the present time Jonas continually is using words that have associations with closeness: until recently all ethics was anthropocentric; 'man' and his basic condition was considered constant in essence.

"The good and evil about which action had to care lay close to the act, either in the praxis itself or in its immediate reach, and were not a matter for remote planning." (p. 4f.)

And in sketching new dimensions of responsibility we find all the time words that have associations with distance:

"No previous ethics had to consider the global condition of human life and the far-off future, even existence, of the race." (p. 10)

These new circumstances make 'old imperatives' outdated and enforce 'new imperatives'. Courage in time of war, for example, will be less important, and there arises a value of maximal information about the long-term consequences of our collective actions and a value of a new sobriety in our consumer's habits.[11] We don't have any more faith in nature taking care of itself. Hölderlin, who by the way played frequently with the themes of closeness and distance, was moved by this faith when he wrote:

Near is
And hard to grasp the God.
But when we are in danger, that what saves us
Is growing also.[12]

The new danger threatening us forces us to reflect on a higher level that separates itself from the obvious schemes of interpretation of the theory of reflective equilibrium.[13] From this follows, according to Jonas:

"A state of emergency, comparable to a state of war,

can be declared, in which some normally inviolable prohibitions and taboos are set aside." (1987, p. 124)

One could say of traditional ethics that is bound up with the names of Hegel, Gadamer and Rawls, that its main task consists in *bringing closer* practical problems. Confronted with questions about the anonymity of sperm donors, about the regret of a surrogate mother after having signed the contract, about the ethical aspects in producing an ideal human being, one loses track nearly immediately: in virtue of what would one rather decide one way instead of the other? As far as moral philosophers have a certain familiarity with analogous problems they can, by considering the similarities and differences between these problems and the novel one, make disappear somewhat the strangeness of the novel case. In this way they can prepare the way for a responsible decision. In the play of closeness and distance the emphasis is here on closeness. Confronted with the fragility of nature and humankind moral philosophers can also set themselves the task of enlarging the distance between us and the problems we are facing. They can do so by making explicit the frames of interpretation that we are using in dealing with our practical problems and that we never put in doubt because of their very familiarity. If the questions facing us are in essential respects so novel that the familiar frames are of no help to us, then the emphasis of the play of closeness and distance is on *distance*.

The play of closeness and distance can even exceed the limits of ethics and force us to answer metaphysical questions. Hans Jonas, too, has noted this. Of his first imperative: that there be a mankind, he says:

31

"With this imperative we are, strictly speaking, not responsible to the future human individuals but to the *idea* of Man, which is such that it demands the presence of its embodiment in the world. It is, in other words, an ontological idea. (...) The first principle of an 'ethic of futurity' does not itself lie *within* ethics as a doctrine of action (within which thereafter all duties toward future beings belong), but within metaphysics as a doctrine of being, of which the idea of Man is a part." (1984, p. 43f.)

He gives concrete form to this ontological idea when he ponders the arguments in favour of and the arguments against cloning human beings. By cloning a human being one would consciously repeat the unique character of a human being, which would entail a 'metaphysical rupture with the normative "essence" of man' (1987, p. 197). Then, it would be true to say:

"The existence of humankind for its own sake looses its ontological basis." (1987, p. 199)

In these circumstances ethics would be superseded by a metaphysical change in the essence of man. I will not examine in detail the thoughts of Hans Jonas on this subject, I only point out that even in an applied ethics, one stumbles at metaphysical problems in the end, and this in a field where one would least expect it to happen.

At the end of my paper I would like to return to the idea of a concrete ethics. The requirement that a philosophical ethics is 'concrete', bears witness to

"... a common prejudice that the science of philosophy is merely concerned with abstractions, with vacuous generalities; intuition, our empirical self-consciousness, our self-concept, the experience of living, on the contrary, supposedly is what is in itself concrete, determinate, and rich. (...) it is the task of philosophising to show against understanding that the true, the idea, does not exist in empty generalities but in a general that is in itself the particular and the determinate. If the true is abstract, then it is untrue. (...) Philosophy is most inimical to the abstract, and leads back to the concrete."[14]

Who wrote this? Indeed, good old Hegel, who both at the beginning and the end of this paper can provide us with beautiful and applicable quotations. He could even write – and this is meant as giving comfort to those who practise concrete ethics:

"With mere abstractions or formal thoughts (...) philosophy has nothing to do at all, but only with concrete thoughts."[15]

By way of summary, I repeat that one can conceive of applied ethics as a play of closeness and distance. If one stresses the aspect of *distance*, then this leads to an attitude of openness and experiment towards our own lives: we don't know exactly what we are and what we want to be, so let's experiment by exploring all the possibilities given to us by, for example, technology. If one stresses the aspect of *closeness*, then this leads to a conserving attitude: we do know rather well what we are and what we want to be, so let's not run after every novel possibility as it turns up. This play of closeness and distance so conceived does not characterize just ethics, but it characterizes a fundamental trait of our existence as human beings.

Notes:

1. My thanks are due to Herman Slangen for translating the Dutch original into English. Unless otherwise stated, the translations from German texts are mine.

2. G.W.F. Hegel, 'Wer denkt abstrakt?' [1807], in: *Werke in zwanzig Bänden*, 2, Frankfurt/M, 1970, p. 575ff.

3. The distinction between technical knowledge and ethical knowledge is made by H.-G. Gadamer in *Wahrheit und Methode*, Tübingen, 1965, p. 298ff.

4.'Unzuhandenheit', *Sein und Zeit*, Tübingen, 1963, p.73.

5. *Nicomachean Ethics*, 1095 a 6. (tr. W.D. Ross, rev. by J.O. Urmson).

6. P.J.M. Van Tongeren interprets ethics as hermeneutics of moral experience, *Moraal, recht, ervaring*, Nijmegen, 1990.

7. In the meantime Theo van Willigenburg has been elaborating the 'network model', that he and Robert Heeger introduced two years ago for the Societas Ethica ('Justification of Moral Judgements: A network Model', in: *Societas Ethica, Jahres-bericht 1989*, p. 53ff.). See *Inside the Ethical Expert: Problem Solving in Applied Ethics*, Kampen, 1991.

8. G.W.F. Hegel, *Phänomenologie des Geistes*, Hamburg, 1952, p. 29 (tr. Walter Kaufmann).

9. 'Justification of Moral Judgements: A Network Model', p. 60.

10. Hans Jonas, *The Imperative of Responsibility*, Chicago & London, 1984, p. 3.

11. Hans Jonas, *Technik, Medizin und Ethik*, Frankfurt/M, 1987, p. 53ff.

12. 'Patmos', in: *Sämtliche Werke*, Berlin und Darmstadt, 1963, p. 328.

13. This point is made by G.A. van der Wal, 'Toegepaste ethiek tussen reflexie en probleemoplossing', MS Rotterdam, 1992.

14. G.W.F. Hegel, *Vorlesungen über die Geschichte der Philosophie*, I, in: *Werke in zwanzig Bänden*, 18, Frankfurt/M, 1971, p. 43.

15. G.W.F. Hegel, *Enzyklopädie der philosophischen Wissenschaften 1830*, Hamburg, 1959, § 82.

About the author:
Dr. F.C.L.M. Jacobs is Associate Professor in Philosophy of Law and Ethics - University of Amsterdam, the Netherlands (Department of Law)

Four Ways of Leaving the Ivory Tower Perspectives on Research in Applied Ethics

Jan Vorstenbosch

Introduction

The problem I want to discuss, somehow reminds me of the story of the man who met the right woman at the right time at the wrong place, because her husband was the barkeeper.

It seems to be the right time, even high time, for applied ethics, considering the many complex ethical problems that have emerged in our societies in the last two decennia, especially in (or with regard to) medicine, science, business and technology. And so applied ethics seems to be the right party to embrace for philosophers and ethicists, who do not close their eyes for the real world. But the problem is to find the right place for the rendez-vous. At the universities, in philosophic circles, applied ethicists are confronted with philosophers and theologians who look suspiciously on what seems to be the 'abduction' of traditional moral philosophy, if not a 'selling out' of its intellectual ideals to the profane world. In more practical contexts applied ethicists meet with social scientists who have their own, often rather positivistic, view on 'values'. This view seldom is very encouraging for normative ethics. And, of course, 'out there' there are everywhere the know-all and do-all practitioners, who have an unshakeable trust in the way they have solved their moral

36

problems from old times on (or even see no problem at all in what they do).

However, this may be a too competitive view of the situation. After all, leaving personal and professional feelings of envy aside, in each of these contexts there is something valuable to be found for applied ethics. We may even say that applied ethics as a discipline came into existence when the walls between philosophy (theology), (social) science and practical moral experience were pulled down. But pulling down walls is easier than building a new house in which one can live and work together. Interdisciplinarity is called for, but more often than not it is only a slogan, not much of a reality.

In this paper I will try to offer some ideas for discussion on the question how the applied ethicist, who is willing to leave the ivory tower of academic ethics, can define and develop his position and task with regard to practical moral problems, especially in so far as research (and not education or counseling) is concerned.

Applied ethics: some preliminary remarks

Usually applied ethics is defined on the basis of its problems and themes, as a reflective activity that is concerned with concrete moral and ethical problems, differing from philosophical ethics only by the fact that it is less fundamental and theoretical. From the perspective of research and the programming of research this definition will not do. We need a starting-point that gives a more systematic and coherent basis to the discipline. In my own view a possible and fruitful starting-point can be found in the notion of 'practices'.[1] Practices are coherent and complex forms of human activities that derive their cohesion and meaning from ends and goods that are internal to that activity. Examples of practices are science, technology, law, politics, philosophy and economics. Practices have a relative autonomy and generate a particular kind of rationality. Applied ethics then is concerned with concrete problems that find their origin in the succesful – all too succesful – development of certain practices like science, economics and technology. These developments have farreaching ethical consequences for society. These consequences are often difficult to assess. First because of the uncertainty that goes with novel and unprecedented situations. But secondly because they challenge the existing morality in a more direct way. They challenge the cultural and moral values that surround institutions like parenthood, marriage, community, politics, and activities like care, labor and sexual behaviour. In short, they jeopardize certain values by which society as such is identified. On both counts, these developments require considerable conceptual, interpretive and argumentative effort. This explains the need for applied ethics.

Given this starting-point, there are certain implications for research in applied ethics that speak for themselves. I will mention four of them. It is inevitable, when we take applied ethics serious, that

(1) ethicists not only must know more about practical problems, but as far as possible must see, face and

experience these problems in practice; without this experience they will have nothing valuable to contribute to practical discussions;

(2) ethicists must pay attention to empirical data that often bear heavily on the stating and solving of ethical problems;

(3) ethicists must pay attention to scientific 'background'-theories that contribute to the understanding of these problems, especially to the understanding of their origins and implications;

(4) cases will get a more prominent place in research in ethics, especially reallife cases (and not the fictitious cases that function as counterexamples for the refutation of ethical theories).[2]

It is not one of these points that I want to put under discussion, at least not in a direct way. My theme will be the question what must be the purpose and object of research in applied ethics.

On this matter, I want to present and explore four options. My main thesis - which I cannot substantiate in this short paper but only offer for discussion - is that these options have strong implications for research, not only for setting research-priorities, but also for the methods of research in applied ethics. These implications are mainly due to the fact that the options are based on certain assumptions concerning ethical theory and moral decision-making in practice, and more specifically concerning the relation between the two.

For reasons of clarity I'll start with namegiving. I will call the four options respectively the Sophist option, the Socratic option, the Platonic option and the

Aristotelian option. As can be seen from these titles, the discussion that applied ethics provokes, is not new.[3] Although the explicit demand from the side of society for ethicists – and even the name 'ethicist' itself – is of recent date, the problems that confront philosophers when they respond to this demand are not so new. They originate in the problematic relation between theory and practice, and in the reflexive attitude that is 'natural' to the philosopher. This attitude makes it impossible to ignore the precarious relation between the making of a theory and the making of practical choices. Intellectual integrity is one of the central virtues of this attitude and it 'forbids' philosophers to close their eyes for the contingencies that characterize opinions and policies on practical matters, including of course their own opinions. Nevertheless, I think that ethicists can contribute to the discussions and decisions, precisely because of their (self-)consciousness with regard to these contingencies.

I will describe the four options in a concise manner, perhaps now and then too sketchy and without necessary qualifications. I hope this will not distract the reader from the essence of the different options.

1. *The Sophistic option: the improvement of the rationality of public debate and decision-making as the object of research*

Central to the Sophistic option is the view that moral argument – and the presentation of moral argument in practice – builds on certain technical abilities of a logical and rhetorical nature. 'Rhetorical' is not used here in its modern pejorative sense, but in the positive (or at least neutral sense) the word had in the Classical and Mediaeval world, as the name of an art: the art to state and defend one's opinion and arguments in a persuasive and convincing way before a certain audience. In Antiquity, the comparison of ethics with a 'craft' or an 'art is a standing topic in the discussion on the relation between ethics and practice. Ethical and political decision-making are seen as human practices in which the participants put forward their views and proposals with regard to the good life and the good society. In the view of the Sophists, the truth of these (normative) views is not to be found outside the debat – in some scientific or philosophical theory –; it is to be found in the public debate itself, in the exchange of opinions and arguments and finally in the making of a well-reasoned choice or the reaching of a decision. This process has to be regulated in a such a way that all people affected can have their say.

The most famous classical sophists like Protagoras and Gorgias appear in the Dialogues of Plato as advocates of what we can call a humanistic relativism. Human beings indeed are the measure of all things. And ethics and politics are processes in which and by which practical solutions are sought for the problems that inevitably arise when human beings are confronted with perennial problems like those of justice, order, relations with 'outsiders', and particularly conflicts between themselves. We can recognize this sort of relativism – which is certainly not an absolute relativism – in much of modern democratic theory. The idea behind this theories is that -when there's no grand theory that can lay a definite claim to undisputed truth and when the human predicament is one of fallibility – the important thing is to organize society in such a way that this fundamentel openness is acknowledged in open institutions and in the virtues we develop.

Applied ethicists who subscribe to the normative assumptions of this Sophistic option and involve themselves with the process of discussion and decision-making can contribute to the improvement of this process at least in the following two ways.

Firstly, by concentrating their reflections on the specific normative assumptions of practices like politics, law, science and economics. These assumptions undoubtedly have a heavy influence on the course of the political process, but often remain implicit. The applied ethicist can contribute to the quality and rationality of the public debate on ethical problems by making these assumptions explicit and by finding ways to mediate between these different normative discourses: maybe the ethicist can play the role of an interpreter and make people understand each other (and maybe even themselves) better.[4]

The second task in which research in applied ethics can contribute to the democratic process is by promoting sound reasoning, and by further developing arguments and reasons. Sometimes the ethicst can (and maybe ought to) secure a 'dialogical' balance between different positions on practical questions by taking the cause of the 'weaker' party. This balance will enable citizens to make their choices on practical matters on a fair presentation of all the arguments available.[5]

2. The Socratic option: the study of power, interests and ideology as the object of research

The Sophistic option implies to a certain extent acceptance of the way practices and institutions have evolved and in any case an engagement with the democratic political process. It is a move in the direction of the 'working-place' of politics and away from the academy (It is no coincidence that the classical Sophists travelled around). The Socratic option is more radically critical, also to the democratic process. Central to this option is the critical task of the philosopher with regard to all established institutions and opinions. The engagement of the ethicist ought to be with thinking, with rationality and with reflection and not with the making of policies, at least not in a direct way. Autonomy, freedom and independency are conditions for exercising criticism. The road the Sophist takes out of the ivory tower, a road which commits him to the improvement of the public debate, puts this autonomy in danger, because practical debates and the decision-making process have their own logic and dynamics. The constraints of these practices influence the posing of the ethical questions and they certainly weigh heavily on the relevance and presentation of the outcome of the thinking-process.

The function of the ethicist is not to help practitioners by construing better arguments, but to irritate them (Socrates compared himself to a gadfly), by permanently questioning their opinions, reasons and justifications. The purpose of applied ethics is one of 'deconstructing' practices and established opinions. Its purpose is to lay bare the ideological structure and aspects of the social debate on practical ethical problems. Especially the standpoints and justifications of representatives of 'dominant' practices like science, economics and technology often hide the contingent normative choices and presumptions that inform them. This hiding is not a conscious activity from the part of spokesmen. Most times it is a consequence of the fact that, being dominant, the opinions have the appearance of realism and even inevatibility.

Names that come to mind in relation to these option are those of Nietzsche and Foucault, whose critical reflections, commentaries and theories on western society and modern instutions have won many followers in the last twenty years. But it's only recently that these ideas and approaches are beginning to be applied to the concrete moral problems and themes of our society. It is not clear what will be the practical consequences and effects of these applications. In theory, this model seems to be the ideal one for the applied ethicist. It combines the traditional intellectual virtues of the philosopher with the advantages of practical liberties. The ethicists can select themes, opinions and arguments as he thinks fit, and comment on them in a way that is free from interests, promises and expectations. But one of the problems of the Socratic option may be that criticism itself is never without its own presuppositions and practical effects. Concentration on the ideology of 'the others' sometimes makes one blind for one's own presuppositions and the effects of one's activities.

3. The Platonic option: the application of ethical theory as the object of reseach in applied ethics

The Platonic option builds on the most straightforward deductive model of application. Central to it is the idea that there is a substantial (and true) ethical theory, that in principle – although not without the usual difficulties of application like correct information and interpretation of the facts etc. – can be applied to concrete situations and problems. In time, these applications will lead to the solving of moral problems. One way this model can be brought into a formula for research is by using the classical syllogism. The maior states the normative principle, that is backed up by a theory, and the minor indicates the significant empirical and practical conditions that have to be taken account of, to realize practical 'problem-solving' in applied ethics. Research in applied ethics, then, should concentrate on the logical relations between the premises, and on the interpretation of the minor.

This option is not to be confused with what is sometimes called the 'engineering-model' in discussions on applied ethics. The engineering-model says that the work of the applied ethicist can be compared with that of an engineer who 'simply' carries out in a professional way orders for clarification and argumentation, given by other people. Besides the fact that this comparison seems to me a simplification of the work of an engineer (and of course of the ethicist), the Platonic option is precisely marked out by the fact that the ethicist has not or at least not only an executive task, but a directing one. He (or she) has a 'legislative', rule-giving function in the process of decision-making.

A relatively pure and outspoken example of this option is given by the practices of party-ideologists in the former marxist-leninist states. Few, however, will take this example serious in the present situation. Of much greater significance is the fact that some ways in which utilitarian theory is worked out, seems to be based on this option, at least in their structure. The greatest well-being of the greatest number can serve as a ruling idea, an idea that in recent times has been refined in its application by the sciences of economics (welfare-theory) and psychology.[6] The applied ethicist has to take his example from the Ideal Observer, who reaches the right moral conclusion in a situation, because he has all information about the consequences for well-being and judges disinterestedly and logically impeccable. To this ideal objective conclusion the ethicist can and must try to contribute, in cooperation with the relevant sciences and practices like medicine, economics, politics that specialize in one aspect of the phenomenon of human (and animal) well-being. The technocratic ring of this approach is unmistakable, but on the other side it cannot be denied that the utilitarian aspects of ethical questions often are the most evident, and give an easy access to a broader discussion.

4. *The Aristotelian option: reflection on human ethos and interpretation of experiences as the object of research*

Central to the Aristotelian option is the idea that human societies in general, and what I have earlier called (following MacIntyre) practices in particular, are defined and structured by their 'ethos', a coherent scheme of norms, values, motives and virtues that gives substance, meaning and orientation to human actions and reactions.[7] This ethos makes it possible to understand and judge the ethicality of actions and the moral worth of persons. Explicit moral 'rules' make out only one aspect of this ethos and probably not the most important one. Most of it is to be found in attitudes, motives, manners, reactions and experiences that 'speak for themselves' in a certain culture or context. The task of the ethicist is to make explicit and articulate this ethos and interpret the moral experiences that develop on the basis of this ethos. Critical reflection on a particular ethos, and normative argument with regard to the way the ethos works out, is not excluded, but it has to take account of the particularity and diversity of practices, their particular presupposition, purposes and nature. When the constraints implied by the ethos, are not taken into account, criticism will have an abstract and 'external' ring and will be of no consequence in practice.

In modern society, however, there is no homogeneous ethos. There is a plurality of 'ethos' of different forms and origins (class, profession, life-style, religion) not only between persons and groups but often in one and the same person as well (modern man lives with more than two souls in his breast). The moral experience of people is shattered, diffuse and 'troubled'. In this situation, the purpose of applied ethics should be the interpretation and reconstruction of moral experiences that people have with regard to the practical developments and innovations that science, medicine and economics initiate in an uninterrupted way. Applied ethics should conceive of itself as a hermeneutics of moral experience, a 'reading' and explication of the meaning that the feelings and reactions of people with regard to the novel situations and problems, have.[8]

Conclusion

The description of these four options for research in applied ethics is far from complete. It is sketchy and tentative. There may also be other options that lead to a more promising framework for discussion. As can be concluded already from a first survey, these four options certainly do not exclude each other. Indeed, there may be a natural inclination to combine all these options (or the important elements of each of them) in an 'ideal' research-program for applied ethics. However, to give in to this inclination may be less profitable than a strategy which concentrates on the differences, and tries to determine the value of each approach in relation to moral problems in practice.

What is needed in any case, is a more precise characterization of these options, their presuppositions and implications, to get a clearer picture of the consequences for research and of the strong and weak points of each of them. It is not possible to argue for one of these options without attending to the central questions of ethics and especially its relation with practical morality. I think that, to be true to its origin and to be ready for its future, applied ethics has to be combined with a permanent (meta-)reflection on its purposes, its presuppositions and its effects on society. It's my hope that this paper has provided some input for this reflection.

Notes:

1. For this notion see: A. MacIntyre, *After virtue, a study in moral theory*, Duckworth, London, 1981, p. 175

2. For this point see, A. Jonsen and S. Toulmin, *The abuse of casuistry*, Berkeley, Un. of California Press 1988, and T. van Willigenburg, *Inside the ethical expert. Problem solving in applied ethics*, Kampen, Kok Pharos Publishing House, 1991, chapter VI.

3. From the way I work out the options that go under these names, it can easily be seen that they are not meant as interpretations of the theories and ideas of the (historic) Sophists, Socrates, Plato and Aristoteles. The most that can be claimed is that they bear a certain and loose relation if not to the theories, then at least tot the practice of these philosophers. The presentation of the options is only meant as a first step in a discussion that to my mind is worth to be carried on.

4. I think of the work of Jurgen Habermas and Karl-Otto Apel as important ways of research in this area.

5. This second task will be the way in which most of the research in applied ethics will be developed and carried out: in relation to the actual debate on specific questions, and especially in relation to the 'bottle-necks' in the debate.

6. See R.M. Hare, 'The rol of philosophers in the legislative process', in: R.M. Hare, *Essays on political morality*, London, 1988. It is not without significance that Hare in his monography on Plato (R.M. Hare, *Plato*, Oxford UP, 1982) presents a very balanced view on the fundamental ideas of Plato's political philosophy and is even sympathethic to Plato's view of the relation between theory and practice (although not to Plato's metaphysical theory).

7. With a term of Hegel we could call this ethos 'Sittlichkeit'.

8. To mention only a few relevant authors under this heading, I'll think of Dietmar Mieth (for instance, D. Mieth, *Die neue Tugenden: ein ethisches Entwurf*, Dusseldorf, Patmos Verlag, 1984) en Martha Nussbaum (M. Nussbaum, *The fragility of goodness*, Cambridge UP, 1986).

About the author:

Dr. J. Vorstenbosch is senior-researcher in Ethics at the University of Utrecht - The Netherlands (Department of Philosophy and Center for Bioethics and Health Law)

The Turn to Applied Ethics

Practical Consequences for Education

Introduction

Has the turn to applied ethics influenced the aim and content of our education-programs in ethics, and, if so, in what respect? How may students in ethics be prepared for their future tasks and challenges? How to discuss a concrete moral problem when the reality of this problem is no part of the reality of the students? Can we teach students to think competently about moral dilemmas without, at least, a very real sense of how other people feel when they have to face or live with the choice? How to bring moral reality, with which apllied ethics is concerned, into the classroom?

Preston Covey goes into these questions by reflecting on his own experiences and efforts to develop vehicles for vicarious experience; vehicles for importing the realities of engagement into the 'ivory-tower classroom'. As a teacher, he observed that in typical case-discussions (who gets the dialysis machine? should the patient be allowed to die? etc.) students show little sense of the predicaments of other people, but also that they often take leave of their own sensibilities and fail to appreciate their own predicaments. Using films or thought-exepriments may help to confront students with the richness and emotionality of a case, and to stimulate their imagination of what it is in reality to decide, e.g., who should get the kidney treatment.

Trying to bring reality into the classroom, however, leads to the crucial question what difference it makes for ethical reflection (which is what students have to learn) if one is aware of the attitudes, feelings and experiences which play a role in real-life cases. What difference does this confrontation with reality make for the papers student have to write?

Recalling some of his own fascinating educational experiments, Covey provides for a tentative answer:

"One thing that can come from intimate engagement with any human predicament is wonder; another is humility; another is intellectual motivation; another is confounding emotion, which plays havoc with our ideals of clear-sighted, so-called 'objective' detachment."

At Carnegie Mellon University, Preston Covey has developed and uses computer-based interactive video for ethics teaching. The advantage of interactive video is its combination of visual experience (extending the moral imagination) and computer interaction. The viewer is challanged to type in reactions and he has control over the information resources which the program provides for. Information about one of these intruiging interactive video programmas is added as an appendix.

The Crucible of Experience

Preston K. Covey

The function of a keynote address is to strike a chord, to set a theme, to provoke and focus discussion. My talk is about practical consequences of the applied turn in ethics for education. These are legion; so I must be selective. My focus will be the neglected empirical dimension of ethics, what I call "the crucible of experience". I leave out of account the complementary theoretical, conceptual, and analytical apparatus of ethics.

Ethics has two complementary modes: detachment and engagement. Each admits of kinds and degrees. Metaphorically speaking, if detachment is a function of the head, engagement is a function of head, heart and viscera. At the extremes, engagement typifies moral experience at first hand, while detachment typifies the theoretical turn in ethics, which examines moral experience at some distance.

Albert Jonsen offers other useful metaphors for contrasting modes of detachment and engagement: the *balloon* riding above the terrain of moral life and the *bicycle* riding its rough and windy roads at close quarters.[1] I am concerned with the experience of the bicyclist and with the need to educate our students with sweaty bicycle tours as with lofty balloon rides and chartography. Unfortunately, a lecture is a format unsuited to my concern. Hot-air lectures fuel balloon rides; it is hard to apprehend from a balloon the experience of the bicyclist. I will have to rely on casuistic anecdotes, analogies, metaphors, personal observations, and rhetorical questions for discussion. I begin with a poem and an ancient pagoda proverb. Poems and proverbs intimate but cannot explicate residues of wisdom from the crucible of experience.

The poem is entitled, appropriately, *Ethics* by Linda Pastan (1980):

In ethics class so many years ago
our teacher asked this question every fall:
if there were a fire in a museum which would you save,
a Rembrandt painting
or an old woman who hadn't many
years left anyhow? Restless on hard chairs
caring little for pictures or old age
we'd opt one year for life, the next for art
and always half-heartedly. Sometimes the woman
borrowed my grandmother's face
leaving her usual kitchen to wander
some drafty, half imagined museum. One year, feeling clever, I replied
why not let the woman decide herself?
Linda, the teacher would report, eschews the burdens of responsibility.
This fall in a real museum I stand before a real Rembrandt, old woman,
or nearly so, myself. The colors
within this frame are darker than autumn,
darker even than winter – the browns of earth,
though earth's most radiant elements burn

through the canvas. I known now that woman
and painting and season are almost one
And all beyond saving by children.

The ancient pagoda proverb reminds us rudely of what
we know all too well:

*A ship of theory, when launched upon the sea of
facts, often sinks.*

How then, shall we teach students of ethics to swim?

"Applied ethics" is really a redundant term, is it not?
What good would ethics do us if it were not applied?
Who ever claimed that it should not be applied? It is a
term that marks a diversified turn in the academy, a
turn not necessarily away from theory, but a turn towards ethical issues that are topical .. in everyday, professional, social or political life; thereby, a heightended
concern with the constaints and realities that compli-
cate ethical judgment; and, often a turn towards in-
creased "clinical" involvement by ethicist .. in mun-
dane, practical, or professional settings.
   I remember well my experience as a graduate student
in 1972. We held informal seminars in which *philosophy* students and faculty would come together with
medical students and faculty to discuss bioethics. We
philosophers were constantly being told, politely or
rudely, that we knew nothing about the hard realities of
medical practice. This was correct; we had no experience in the exigencies and contingencies that plague
medical judgment; our competence and credibility were,

therefore, commensurately compromised.

In the last quarter century, bioethics has matured as a genuinely collaborative interdisciplinary field. One sign of this maturity is the emergence of clinical models for applied ethics, the medical clinic being the prime analogue. Today, for example, more medical students participate in what are called "ethical rounds" and more ethicists participate in traditional clinical rounds. A medical clinic, unlike medical school, is a place where exigent life-and-death decisions have to be made, in real time, under the duress of uncertainty, with real consequences and costs at stake. But clinical practice presupposes medical schooling, detailed domain knowledge, as well as hands-on experience. Ethical problem-solving in clinical settings require knowledge of facts as well as experience with rudely urgent realities that allow little time for reflection. This is all widely recognized by professional ethicists.

Of course, bioethics is not the only field in which the application or maturity of ethical wisdom requires experimential engagement. Every domain requires it. But an ethicist's mode and degree of clinical experience can vary – from deliberating binding policy on an ethics committee to accompanying physicians on grand rounds, from the training of practitioners in the field to taking the training oneself, from being what ethnographers call a "partcipant-observer" to being a mere observer. Samuel Gorovitz, a philosopher, for his recent book *Drawing the Line: Life, Death, and Ethical Choices* spent several weeks in intimate observation at a Boston hospital. Kenneth Schaffner, a philosophy Ph.D., completed medical school for an M.D.degree.

Different problems and different ambitions in applied

ethics will call for different modes of engagement, and mileage will vary. For example, one of my specialities is the law and ethics of deadly force. I found the philosophic literature in this field, and in police ethics generally, to be preachy, scholastic, vapid, and obviously uninformed by any experience in the field. Unlike bio ethics, police ethics, as an applied and interdisciplinary field, is in its infancy. I gravitate towards neglected problems, so I decided to adopt this field as a proving ground for how applied ethics might be done. For me, this means getting as close to the front lines as possible, a version of the "practitioner-observer" approach. The domain of practice that I selected was training in the use of force. Combat training is the next best (or next worst) thing to combat, for understanding the realities of lethal confrontation. So I sought certification as an instructor in the use of deadly force.

This field implicates all the dimensions of applied ethics: exigent decisions under uncertainty, competing rights and duties, vice and virtue, insitutional realities, cultural conflict, politics, sociology, law, policy-making, and grave social disorders. My practical research culminated just last week with the completion of 500 hours of training. I have now undergone more (and more advanced) training in weaponcraft, threat management, the dynamics of lethal encounters, and the use of force than most sworn police officers. I will continue to research the ethical issues in the use of force by conducting training myself. The training field is for me one laboratory, one crucible of experience.

But what is the source of my compulsion to go this far? And what will I do with what I learn?

One thing that I do with what I learn is develop vehicles for vicarious experience, vehicles for importing the realities of engagement into the groves of academe, into the ivory-tower classroom. One such vehicle is film or video. Another is computer-based interactive video. An interactive videodisc is something that must be shown and seen, not described. But I can give you a vague idea.

At Carnegie Mellon University we are developing inter-active videodisc on obscenity and art censorship, conflict resolution techniques, struggles with the decision to give birth or abort, and one on the use of force. The latter is called *Excessive Force? The case of Iowa v. Willems*. Each of the interactive video projects serves the goal of reflective engagement; each poses questions on which there is general controversy; each presents compelling documentary case studies, 'rabbit holes', as it were, leading into a complex underground warren of issues that begin an odyssey in which student explorers, like Alice in Wonderland, must struggle to maintain their own bearings; each provides a curriculum or database of resources for charting the complex and controversial terrain.

For example, the videodisc on the use of force presents the case of Corporal Randall Willems, a police officer on trial for shooting an unarmed man. The central question of this real-life drama is whether Willems is guilty of *excessive* force. The underlying ethical question, of course, is what conditions can ever *justify* the use of deadly force. Unlike a linear film, the videodisc environment will include an indexed data-base of statutory law, case law, departmental policy, empirical studies and other case-study material that bear om the use of force in American society. The pedagogical design of the odyssey through this material is dialectical: whether the student gravitates towards a "guilty" or "not guilty" verdict, contrary evidence is presented and her legal and ethical judgment is interrogated. The verdict in the Willems case is not the point; the point is rather to put the student's judgment under duress and to explore, in very specific and concrete terms, the law and ethics of deadly force decisions. You might imagine, by analogy, how useful it would be to have an interactive frame-by-frame analysis of the videotape of the Rodney King beating in Los Angeles, with the relevant legal arguments and case law indexed at your fingertips in a computer database. So, one thing I do with my training is apply it to the design of educational environments for university students as well as to professional in-service training.

My involvement with the technology was motivated in turn by my experience and frustration as a teacher of applied ethics. Let me sketch that experience with a few anecdotes.

My students, by virtue of callow youth or worldly ignorance, were good at distancing themselves from the hard problems and realities of moral live. Their modes of detachment were a challenge to overcome.

I remember well a curious report from our Student Advisory Center many years ago: a majority of the freshman in the required ethics course complained that they were bored with the topic of abortion. *Why?*, I asked. The most common reason was: *We studied that subject in high school already*. What a curious idea, I thought. Are we such miserable teachers? Are the isues

so removed from their experience? Is abortion too un-
real and unimaginable? Or to real and painfully conflicted? The dimension of feeling about this issue – feelings that tear people apart, that divide my own society
today indecently over matters of decency – are surely
ones we would not wish any person to suffer. But without a vivid sense of these dimensions of feeling, the
choice situation so laboriously debated cannot competently be assessed. Three questions, then, emerge:

(1) Is there a way to let students see and feel what is at
stake here, the irreducible agonies to be faced, without
actually putting them through the decision itself?

(2) Can we teach students to think competently
about moral dilemmas without, at least a very real
sense of how other people feel when they have to
face or live with the choice?

(3) Is it any wonder that students get bored with abstract
debates about problems that to them are not 'real'?

Not only may callow students have little sense of the
predicaments of other people, but they often take leave
of their own sensibilities and fail to appreciate their
own predicaments. I remember well the day that a student had the temerity in class discussion to object (the
case at issue is irrelevant): *But that would be lying*! A
wave of guffaws rolled out of the back row of football
players, a male chorus announcing to the class their
macho worldly-wise cynicism, *Like, hey, so what?*
What was going on here? A typical lapse. People take
leave of their senses, especially in classrooms; in this

case, the football players took leave of their sense of the stake they have in whether people, as a rule, lie or don't lie. I don't know whether this is a special problem in the philosophy classroom, that students lose touch with what they really care about, but, like any concientious teacher, I looked for ways to counter the phenomenon of detached sensibility.

For one thing, I began using films in class, an obvious strategem, to import a little reality. There was the case of the Downs Syndrome baby with duodenal atresia (blockage of the esophagus). The question was: May the parents deny permission for surgery to correct the blockage, thereby causing their mongoloid infant to die of starvation? This was not the abortion issue, but it was close; and equally removed from the students' own experience, I supposed. The film showed the agony of the parents' decision to withhold surgery, the agony of the infants' slow death by starvation. Film over, lights on, dead silence, no motion to leave. Of course. Who could fail to be moved? At last I had their undivided attention? At last life-and-death issues were no longer boring? This was a topic they hadn't covered in high school? All this was surely true; but there was more than engagement by the dramatic.

For example: in the next class, two days later, I asked the students for their reactions to the film. Most expressed surprise as well as dismay. Surprise at something they had not thought about in reading the case beforehand. Surprise to see how painful it was for the nurses who had to watch that infant die under their care, for two whole weeks. But, I pointed out, we *did* read and talk about the objections of the medical staff to the decision. *Yes, but we didn't realize what that would be like....what it would be like for the nurses.*

The crucial impact here was not just the emotional effect of the film. Rather, it was their surprise, their *discovery* of something they had failed to imagine: the palpability of the nurses' suffering, the compelling interest the nursing staff had in not suffering that infant's death. This discovery detracted nothing from the tragedy for the infant and for its parents. The only lesson, perhaps, was that some things have to be seen and felt to be imagined. No one thought the nurses' interest bore decisively on the case; but all felt it was important to be aware of it. *Why?* I asked. *What difference does it make to be aware of the nurses' feelings if they don't decisively tip the scales in the case?* That, we all agreed, was an intriguing question.

Films were one obvious pedagogical tool; thought-experiments, sometimes know as lies, were another. Another class: the topic was the typical *Who gets the dialysis machine? How should we decide?* The papers I received rehearsed the standard arguments from the readings, pro and con. I told the class that their papers were lackluster, *Time* magazine could do better; facile in their treatment of the cases; unimaginative about what they considered to be relevant or the further information needed to make a decision. In summary, I said, I didn't think they gave a damn about who got the kidney treatment or how.

How is that supposed to make a philosophy paper better? someone asked. A good question. I needed an *experimentum crucis*. So I lied. I told the class that I had gotten the cases from a colleague on the ethics committee at Presbyterian Hospital; that these were real patients, alive today, awaiting a decision on treatment, some of whom, without that treatment, would surely die within weeks or months. I said that these patients had agreed to read the students' papers, and that I was going to give them these papers, with the students names blanked out, for their reaction.

The students were stunned; some were angry. *You can't do that!*, someone said. *Why do you care?*, I asked. *They won't know who you are!* No quick answer to this. *Why do you care?*, I asked again. *We didn't think they were real*, someone said. *What difference does it make?*, I pressed. *Your papers aren't going to decide the case. Wouldn't it be interesting to know what they think? Aren't you curious?*

That's gross! someone said.
So you care about these people's feelings? Of course. *What about who gets the life-saving treatment?* Of course. *If I were to give your papers to the patients or ethics committee, would you want a chance to rewrite them?* Of course. *Why? Do you think anything you might say now will make any difference?* Probably not. *Then why rewrite them? What difference could it make?* That's not the point. *Yes? Well, what is the point?* We all agreed that was an intriguing question; and they would rewrite their papers.

One student asked: *Would you really have done that? Are those really real people?* I said that I wouldn't and they weren't, but asked again if they would like to rewrite their papers anyway.

Yes. *What a reality trip!* someone said. No one questioned why I had lied.

Getting personal, by ad hominem or appeal to emotion, was another tactic for putting students in touch with their sensibilities and predicaments. Ad hominem and 'appeal to emotion' are classic categories of fallacy. This is curious, since most 'fallacies' much of the time are indispensable to all manner of inquiry: where would law courts be without the *ad hominem*? Appeals to emotion are an especially pathetic case of 'fallacy' because susceptibility to emotional appeal is one of the most precious human capacities in moral life. Appeals to emotion are essential to doing ethics; emotions, like moral intuitions, are admissable evidence; we understand, of course, that they are not dispositive or conclusionary. We could use more appeals to emotion in our pedagogy. Case in point – this case might be called "The Sophist Sandbags the Sophomore":

Carl Hempel, the distinguished philosopher of science, was our guest speaker at the joint Carnegie Mellon / University of Pittsburgh Philosophy Club one evening. The topic was dilemmas of free will and determinism.

Carl was having a devil of a time getting one sophomore student, I'll call him Determined, to admit any intuitive appeal whatever for the notion of free will. Determined thought this notion was one of the great gratuitous delusions of the opiated masses. Determined seemed genuinely, if ironically, indignant at the idea that anyone would be weak willed enough to believe in 'free will'. Kindly and patient, Carl tried every angle he could think of to get Determined *to see* the appeal of the idea, *to see* that important consequences followed from its denial ...else we have no dilemma! Determined could only smile indulgently; that was precisely his position: there is no dilemma here; there's just no basis for this fuzzy illusory commody, and rational kind will give it up!

Throughout this discussion, Determined's girl friend was all aglow over his performance and demonstrably affectionate. Determined gloated over her attentions. At one point, the girl gently kissed Determined on his cheek. Determined smiled at her – happy young love, the very picture. At this point, I jumped in. *Determined uh, sorry, but I couldn't – I'm sure we all couldn't – help noticing: Your girl friend is very fond of you, and you of her; she just kissed you. That was nice. You liked that?* Sure. *You think she meant it, to be nice, to show you she likes you, loves you?* Sure. *Do you think she loves you, that's why she kissed you?* Sure. *And you really think she meant it?* Yeh, sure; what do you mean? *You really think her kissing you meant something? You feel it meant something that she felt like kissing you, that she likes to kiss you, that she did kiss you – rather, than, say not kissing you or, say,... sneezing, or say, biting her fingernail? You think this kiss was something she did sincerely, not just something that, say, just happened, like a sneeze or a hiccup or a twitch?* Sure, yeh, sure; what's the deal?

Well, I was just wondering why you, since you are such a hardball determinist, why you feel this thing she did has any more meaning than, say, a leaf falling off a tree....a heart beating its beat...or her chewing her gum....or her not doing these things or....anything else? Can you tell me why you attach special meaning to her kiss, when, in your view, it's just like a billiard ball bouncing off another ball in the great chain of deterministic hardball?

How do you reconcile the meaning you give to her

kiss? Perhaps you give it special meaning because you're determined to do so? Or, perhaps, you feel a little tug, a little compulsion to believe that she did this nice thing, as we opiated fools are wont to say....out of her own, dare I say it...free will?

That was a terrifying moment for me because I didn't know how this sophistic intrusion into the student's personal space would affect him; I didn't know whether he, or she, would feel hurt.

But the plot worked. That does not mean that Determined became a believer in free will; I have no idea about that, nor was that my point. I provided no refutation of determinism, any more than Mr. Johnson refuted skepticism by kicking the stone; I merely induced an experience.

The student suddenly found himself not refuted, but engaged indeed *possessed* – possessed by the common human sense of the ineluctable allure of the idea of 'free will', the common human sense that vague but important things did seem to hang on this fuzzy but strong sensation, things that he deeply cared about, that he could neither exactly explain nor explain away. He was possessed by the palpable sensation of dilemma.

Having monopolized the discussion to this point, he finally said, in response to my rude and playful questions, that he honestly didn't know what to say.

In wonder, we are told, begins philosophy. I believe that this student was simply beginning to suffer wonder.

One thing that can come from intimate engagement

with any human predicament is wonder; another is humility; another is intellectual motivation; another is confounding emotion, which plays havoc with our ideals of clear-sighted, so-called "objective" detachment. Such is live; and that is just the point.

One such thing that the applied turn in ethics means for *professionals* is engagement with the practical and emotional realities that create the problems to which ethics is applied. But then:

(1) Why should education require anything less of our students?

(2) Is what's good for the goose not good for the gosling?

(3) Is not one practical consequence of the applied turn in ethics that our students must be educated as bicyclists as well as balloonists?

(4) As theory founders upon the sea of facts, must we not teach our students to swim in that sea?

(5) Can we hope to teach applications of ethics to students who are devoid of relevant experience and confounding emotion?

Educational media – be they oral, textual, visual, dramatic, or interactive – are all at some remove from life, but they can provide at least a crucible of *vicarious* experience. As Robert Fullinwider[2] has observed:

"If moral learning is essentially by doing then *the central and ongoing resource for moral education is experience, real or vicarious*....[In school] limitations of time, place resources and structure mean that any major broadening of moral experience must come by way of vicariously living through the moral lives of others.... in literature ....history ....Through stories ....[emphasis added]."

Within the confines of the ethics classroom, by art and artifice, we must engage students with the values and predicaments of others, with the sea of facts on which theory founders, with the bicyclist's view of rough terrain, with myriad problems that are "all beyond saving by children" as well as with their own unexamined values and predicaments. For this task, technology provides vehicles analogous to both balloons and bicycles.

At Carnegie Mellon, we resort to modern technology, ironically, to animate an ancient insight into the nature of ethical wisdom. In the so-called 'Golden Age', in the beginnings of the Western philosophic tradition in ancient Greece before Platonic abstraction, one vehicle for *theory* was the *theater*. Universal elements of 'the human condition' were reflected by chorus and convention in the concrete, compeling drama of Greek tragedy and comedy, which, we are told, induced that paradox of human wisdom called "detached engagement".

With this inspiration in mind, we have dubbed our use of interactive video technology "Project THEORIA". *Theoria* (Greek for *theory*) is an allusion to the concept of theory rooted in concrete observation. It plays

70

upon the common etymological root of both *theory* and *theater* in the ancient Greek verb *theorein*: to see, to view, to behold. Projekt THEORIA aims to provide a theater for ethical theory, to bring it to ground in observable, palpable, affective contexts that are rich in the complex reality that any competent theory must first behold in order to explain.

Computer-based interactive video is a hybrid medium that can *complement* traditional visual and narrative media. The advantage of interactive video as a vehicle for delivering vicarious experience is its *combination* of two crucial features of experimental learning:

(1) compelling *visual* experience – like film, but unlike books – to engage the emotions and extend the moral imagination where vivid first-hand experience is lacking;

(2) computer *interaction* to challenge the viewer intellectually, to afford the viewer control over the material, to enable reflection – like books, but unlike film.

Interactive video combines the power of television or film with the interactivity of the computer as well as online access to narrative text; it combines the best of both worlds, as it were, into a unique opportunity for dramatic, lively interaction, and careful reflection; it speaks at once to our senses, our sensibilities and our minds, offering a very 'life like' experiential crucible. These simple capabilities enable the user to become engaged as an active investigator, rather than a passive observer or reader, and to negotiate the hazardous strait between Scylla and Charybdis, between excessive abstraction and confounding emotion, between untethered detachment and unreflective engagement.

Surely, applied ethics, whatever its forms and dimensions, is not an end in itself:

Non scholae, sed vitae dicimus
[Not for school, but for life do we learn]
Epistolea Morales

Notes:

1. 'Of Balloons and Bicycles – Or – The Relationship between Ethical Theory and Practical Judgment', *The Hastings Center Report*, September/October 1991.

2. 'Learning Morality', *The Report* from the Institute for Philosophy & Public Policy, Spring 1988)

About the author:
Prof.dr. Preston K. Covey is Director of the Center for Advancament of Applied Ethics at Carnegie Mellon University, Pittsburg, U.S.A.

Appendix

A Right to Die? The Case of Dax Cowart
– A Video for Ethics –

1. Overview

A Right to Die? The Case of Dax Cowart is an interactive videodisc program developed by the team of Preston Covey, Scott Roberts, Steven Bend and Robert Cavalier of Carnegie Mellon University, in consultation with Dax Cowart.

1.1 Technical details

The control software and interface of Version 1.0 is implemented in three languages in order to run on multiple platforms: (1) PilotPlus, running on an IBM XT/PC, AT, or PS/2 driving a Pioneer 6000 or 4200videodisc player and an IBM InfoWindow Touch Display system, which allows text and graphics to be overlayed onto the video presentation; (2) the cT programming language, running on both Apple Macintosh as well as IBM PS/2 M-Motion platforms enhanced with appropriate video-digitizing boards, which allows the video to run in maipulable windows on a color monitor; and (3) HyperCard 2.0 for Macintosh platform atilizxing both an ordinary black/

white monitor and a color video monitor. The Hyper-Card software was developed by Dr. Joseph Henderson and Matthew Williams of the Interactive Media Lab at the Dartmouth Medical School. Version 1.0 will be published and distributed in 1992-93 by Falcon Software, Inc. (P.O Box 200, Wentworth NH 03282; 203-764-5788).

Earlier versions of *A Right to Die?* won the Best Humanities Software Award in the 1989 EDUCOM/ NCROPTAL Higher Education Software Awards Program (version0.9) and a 1988 Merit Award from the Nebraska Videodisc Design/Production Group (version 0.1). The development of the videodisc program was supported in part by grants from the Claude Worthington Benedum Foundation, the Andrew W.Mellon Foundation, The Pew Memorial Trust, he Alfred P. sloan Foundation, and equipment grants from Online Computer Systems and International Business Machines Corporation. This is dedicated with special gratitude to Dax Cowart and people like him who exemplify moral experience and inquiry in their most plainful forms.

1.2 The famous case of Dax Coward

The program presents the famous and now classic case of Dax Cowart, a victim of severe burns, blindness, and crippling injuries who persists under treatment to insist that he be allowed to discontinue treatment and die. Through interviews with Dax and other principals in the case (his doctors, lawyer, mother, etc.), the user investigates basic ethical issues regarding quality of life, patient interest and rights, the conflicting interest and obligations of medial professionals, etc. Throughout, the user must continually address the central dilemma: Whether Dax should be granted his request to die and what reasons should support the decision. The videodisc program will support several hours of interactive exploration of the issues and case material. It allows the viewer to do this two different modes.

The first mode poses questions in the manner of a Socratically guided inquiry by which the user is led eventually to consider all the facts, issues, and viewpoints in the case. The program branches and questions users in order to challenge their responses with contrary views and visuals.

The program uses these responses to direct the user to apt or challenging branches of inquiry and to query the consistency of an evolving position. When the viewer is asked to make a final judgment about whether or not Dax should be allowed his request to discontinue treatment and die, surprising consequences follow for either choice. When the user exits the program, answers and comments indexed to the program units and video segments can be printed out for review.

The second mode allows the user free access to video archives in which the video segments are organized by both major issues and principals. This more exploratory mode, unencumbered with questions posed by the program, can be used for review or selective browsing of the case material. The user's menu of options is outlined below:

Introduction:	Video montage:	Poses te dilemma and basic task.
Guided Inquiries:	The Facts:	Interactive analysis of the case narrative.
	The Issues:	Interrogation follows each video segment under: The medical Proffesionals' Obligations Pain of treatment Quality of life Issues The Patient's Rights and Capacities
Archives:	Case Summary:	For review.
	The Issues:	Files relevant video segments under each issue.
	The Principals:	Files the video segments under each principal.

1.3 Varied use

In part because of its compelling subject matter in part because of its interactive mode of presentation, this videodisc program has been employed in a wide variety of settings. These have included a nursing department in a community college and an ethics class in a medical school as well as philosophy, rethoric, writing, and general humanities courses at universities. The program has also been used within hospitals and medical schools as a learning tool for medical staff and ethics committees and in a graduate education school seminar on the design of interactive multimedia learning environments.

The videodisc can be used in a number of different ways. It has been used primarily as a stand-alone resource with individual students or small teams of students for sustained investigation of the case study and the issues it presents. The videodisc system has been used with a projector in both large classes and seminar groups as a lecture and discussion aid, similar to the use of slide carousels in the classroom. The videodisc environment is also being used as a case study in multimedia design research and in research of the impact and role of emotion in moral reasoning, where it provides a window on how different people reason and learn about complex, emotionally charged ethical problems in concrete contexts. The videodisc is thus suited to serve as a vehicle for educational research as innovative education.

2. An educational problem

Students have difficulty 'respecting' ethical issues in classroom settings. It is difficult to teach *about* dilemmas in which complex ethical considerations vie for attention and resolution. Moral reflection and imagination require an experiential crucible, an analogue to the scientist's laboratory or the surgeon's theater, rich in palpable complexity that is impossible to ignore, where choices must be made under duress and uncertainty and consequences suffered. The feeling that some problems are not real until they happen to us (a costly formof education) can be obviated by sharper perception of the problems of others. Vicariously sharing others' defeat in the face of problems incapable of clear or felicitous solution, problems of surprising dimensions, undercuts the often facile, judgment reaction that controversial questions raise in both the political arena and the classroom. it is understandably hard for students to perceive problems that they have not experienced.

2.1 Learning through heart and senses

I taught Dax's case, in narrative form, for six years and have taught ethics for two decades. My students had the most difficulty with three dimensions of the enterprise: (1) motivation for the rigors of analysis and arguments on abstract conceptual and theoretical points; (2) the imaginative challenge to identify with the viewpoints of people whose experience or dilemmas they did not happen (yet) in fact to share; and (3) the ability to identify and sort out their own conflicted values. Students have been known to giggle at the suggestion that lying is wrong, deny any notion of 'free will' as if it meant nothing to them, argue that any desire to die reflects only insanity – or, with egually disengenuous perversity, cleave absolutistically to the contrary views. These three difficult challenges are basic requirements for ethical inquiry. (3) and (2) are prerequisites to (1). Vivid experience, direct or vicarious, opens the way to (3) and (2).

At present, I have mainly anecdotal evidence and my own observation that one way to students' minds, in ethics at least, is through their hearts and senses. Robert Coles (*The Call of Stories*), J.Anthony Lucas (*Common Ground) and other's attest the power of human stories at*

78

close quarters to open both our hearts and our minds to controversies that rend our souls and society alike. The content added in the videodisc is visual as opposed to narrative. It poses its own difficulties, the difficulties of opening too many (as opposed too few) channels at once. Some students object that the material is too strong and upsettimng. We must deal with this difficulty. The larger learning context, instructor- and peer-support in the use of the videodisc, like a field trip to clinical settings, is crucial; the total social-instructional environment must be considered. In the meantime, this difficulty is preferable to disrespect for the issues. One apologetic reply is, Such is life – that is just the point.

The study of ethics is too often academic and speculative in the worst senses of those terms. In serious science education we expect students to handle apparatus and process data that is rich in both quantity and quality. In ethics we typically rely on intelletual apparatus alone and demand neither quantity nor quality in the data to be explained. Nor are we accustomed to introducing *hard* or *raw* data onto our studies, being more comfortable with those abstract commodities of detached academic discourse: well-formed propositions, reasons, concepts, and denatured case studies. There are not enough, if our aim is education for life in the wider world rather than life in the privileged and insulted groves of academi.

Consider the analogy: We do not attempt to teach science by acquainting students with 'scientific method' through books and hot-air disputations (even in most high schools). We do not teach scientific theory abstracted from some hands-on experience with how it is constructed. Science education involves not only the theoretical content of science, but also its art, its craft, its texture, its headaches and frustrations. Put another way, we would not think of *credentialing* schientists, engineers, surgeons, or other artists without providing them some hands-on experience with the actual stuff and rude realities of 'real' life practice.

Consider the contrast: Ethics is typically taught by exposing students, through books and hotair disputations, to verbiage. The verbiage is presumably articulate, insightful, and about matters of great concern or practical import. But it is typically occupied with the analysis of abstract ideas about these matters. In life, ethical problems come trammeled with confounding immidiacy, detail, and emotion; whereas the classroom is experientially barren, devoid of the stuff of moral experience, with meager data in minute quantity, problems faintly viewed at grand theoretical distances, and propositions analyzed to a practically impotent fare-thee-well.

2.2 Armchair theory or.....

The problem in the discipline of philosophy that our videodisc addresses is not just that ethics is often poorly taught as a useful reflective discipline for life, as a reflective vessel for moral growth. The abstract, denatured practice of academic study makes for bad, armchair theory as well. Academic ethics is typically preoccupied with its own abstract conceits and grossly underwhelmed by the data and realities of moral experience. It might be fair to say that ethical theory has achieved the maturity of classical mechanics, by virtue of ignoring large confounding dimensions of human experience. This is conspicuously the case in how poorly ethical theory takes account of human emotion and sensibility, problematic forces – and invaluable resources – in moral affairs. Apart from a few classical thinkers (for example Aristotle, Hume) and a recent growing literature (creditable in large part to feminist thinkers and female philosophers), feelings have been disparaged as mere sources of fallacy and bias, forces to be neutralized or overcome in moral reflection.

The limitations of rational decision models are not even as fully acknowledged in ethical theory as they are in economic or political ones. It is perhaps ironic that a recently acclaimed and contentious book, *Passion Within Reason: The Strategic Role of the Emotions,* was written by an economist (Frank, 1988). The functional and evidence-bearing roles of emotion in ethical reasoning requires more critical stydy than it has received in philosophy. *Interactive* environments that elicit confounding feelings can also serve as laboratories for this study, as ours does and will. Philosophers need to become more involved with the empirical dimensions of ethics; for example, observing how learners in fact wrestle with ethical issues under emotional duress. An interactive video environment provides one window on this process.

2.3 The most important commodity for learning: life experience

Too many real-world problems for which we aim to eguip our students are not well captured in books, lectures, or class discussion. These media cannot always *stimulate* the practical realities or *stimulate* the human

sensibilities that motivate and confound political or ethical dilemmas. Typical students lack one important commodity for learning: life experience – or enough of it.
Typical academic sttings lack adequate means to provide
this commodity. In academic terms, the lack is one sufficient *data* and *context* – particular in areas like ethics or
politics, where much of the essential data and context are
perceptual, experiential, even emotional.

Too often students (and teachers) approach the consideration of dilemmas as abstract, academic exercises, devoid of the excruciating perplexities of real life moral
choices. For an example of the descrepancies between
abstract description and palpable perception of relevant
'fact' or 'information' in ethical dilemmas, consider the
case of Dax Cowart: Dax was a young man involved in
a tragic accident that took his sight and left him without the use of his hands. In addition, as part of his burn
therapy, he was for fourteen months subjected to daily,
painful antiseptic washing. Dax asked – indeed, de-
manded – to have the treatments discontinued. This
would certainly result in massive infection and death; a
fact that he knew. The dilemma: Does Dax have a right
to refuse treatments that would certainly save his live,
although they would leave him a blind cripple? Would
his right to die entail a right against some nameable
person who then would be obligated to help him to
die? What do you need to know, consider, and weigh in
orer to decide such an issue?

2.4 Qualitative and affective information

Here is a simple example of the sort of qualitative and affective information that is difficult to convey by non-visual media: The narrative facts of Dax's case tell us that Dax's hands are nearly useless, that his treatment is extremely painfull, that his mother and doctors refuse to release Dax from treatment, contrary to his own articulate demands. The qualitative realities behind these facts are vividly evident in the program's visuals. Visualization conveys a direct sense of crucial questions: *How* useless are Dax's hands? *How* painfull is his treatment? *How* uncertain does the future quality of his life *seem*? How do his mother and doctors *feel* about letting Dax die without treatment? How lucid is Dax? And, as you *see* it, would *you* be willing to take active measures to let or help Dax die? Some problems must be seen to be imagined, to be analyzed responsibly, to be resolved sensitively. Visual material conveys the sort of raw, experiental data required by our moral sensotium for responsible analysis of ethical issues; that is, analysis that is *responsive to* the emotional and practical burdens of all parties to the case.

For six years I presented this case using traditional narrative case study materials. The typical result was that students had difficult 'seeing' and aptly representing the ethical problems and conflicting viewpoints in the case. No surprise. How can we expect them to construct an apt and compelling representation of an ethical problem or viewpoint from a denatured case abstract? The needed but often neglected resource in moral education is palpable, concretely situated experience. As Robert Fullinwider (1988) has observed,

> If moral learning is essentially learning by doing, then *the central and ongoing resource for moral educatuon is experience, real or vicarious...[In school]*

limitations of time, place, resources and structure mean that any major broadening of moral experience must come by way of vicariously living through the moral lives of others...in literature...history ...through stories...[emphasis mine]

The lack of an experiential base for moral education is compounded by our historical ambivalence about the role of emotion in ethical reasoning. A myth perpetrated by conventional wisdom or the typical logic textbook is: We must always deliberate impartially and unemotionally. In actual fact, we do not and we can not, in any strict sense. This is at best a simplstic rule of thumb. Impartially is a formal ideal. In our fallibility, in material reality, we weigh a plurality of partialities and interests. The question is how we do so, or best learn to we weigh a plurality of partialities and interests. The question is how we do so, or best learn to do so, appropriately. Emotions are, literally, *informative*. Our sensibilities inform our moral perceptions and are informed in turn by pragmatic experience beyond anything that we can fully analyze. Anger can be *prima facie* evidence of wrongdoing. Fear may carry an accurate perception of risk or threat. Emotional hurt, like physical pain, may accurately signal important harm. Our emotions alert us to the very commodities we seek to protect by any system of moral rules: our interests, our values, what-all. upon reflection, we care about.

2.5 Integration of emotion and reason

One challenge, the challenge we attempt to adress with the videodisc, is to accomodate and integrate both

84

emotion and reason in moral education. The consequences of a decision, action, policy, or general rule
cannot be assessed without a vivid representation of the
interest of others. The trick is not simply to learn to put
yourself in the other person's 'shoes' or circumstance,
but to learn to put yourself in another's 'skin', perspective or feelings. Knowing what *I* would do in your situation does not necessarily let me understand what **you**
happen to feel in your situation. Ethics demands more
intellectual and emotional work on my part. To repre-
sent an ethical issue, to perceive that there exists an
ethical problem, requires an appreciation of what is at
stake, of the threatened values and interests of al affected stakeholders. This is essential even to our most theoretical speculations as well as to our deliberations in
the most concrete of situations.

We may situate this task of moral education in the larger context of our hopes for moral and cultural
progress, characterized by Richard Rorty as progress *in
the direction of greater human solidarity.* In *Contingency, Irony, and Solidarity,* Rorty characterizes the root of
huamen solidarity in a way that is perfectly apposite to
the intended function of the videodisc about Dax Cowart and the other stake-holders in his troubling case, as
a *matter of inmaginative indentification with the details
of others'lives* (Rorty,1989). One problem addressed by
the videodisc is how to facilitate such imaginative iden-
tificaton and its attendant empathic skills, to serve as
an object lesson on the path to greater humen solidarity
in a pluralistic world.

3 An Educational Solution

A Right to Die? The Case of Dax Cowart is one of a series of videodiscs conceived under the title *Project theoria.* As an acronym, *theoria* stands for "Testing Hypotheses in Ethics/Esthetics: Observation, Realism, Imagination, and Affect". One goal of the project is to vivify issues in ethics with visually rich case material. Project *theoria* aims to capture and facilitate the original Greek root of both "theater" and "theorie", the act of reflective observation. The aim is to design a theater wherein viewpoints or bias, hypotheses or theories about human values can be challenged by one's own direct bservation.

With all its powers, the computer cannot contribute much to the learning of open-ended subjects ike moral philosophy... fields of knowledge that cannot be reduced to formal rules and procedures. Derek Bok's allegation (1985) is certainly true in its second claim. And the second claim may seem good reason for believing the first, if one's model is the computer as expert system or automated tutor, the computer as teacher. But if one takes seriously the model of the computer as navigational aid and experiential learning environment (as persuasively described and positively assessed by Bok in the self-same paper), then the first claim hardly follows. The computer can provide new channels to moral experience, new stimuli to moral imagination, as well as new opportunities for reflection on that experience.

The contribution to moral education that our videodisc attempts to exemplfy is a dimension of moral learning

86

that is lacking in typical academic study: access to the rich, affecting data of 'real life' dilemmas that reveal our own conflicted values and allow us to identify with those of others. In *Teaching Values in College,* Richard Morril (1981) provides a sensible framework for values education, consisting of three dimensions: *values analysis,* the explicit articulation of the values, principles, and concepts that underlie out value judgments and choices (a priority of traditional ethics courses); *values consciousness,* where crucial components are selfknowledge (discovering and 'owning' one's own often inchoate, contesting values) and empathy (coming to identify with or understand others' values); and *values criticism,* raising questions about the values posited or discovered (another priority of traditional ethics courses).

Values consciousness is a difficult objective to define and attain in academic settings, but it is crucially material to the analytic and critical dimensions of moral learning. Our videodisc aims to provide a model environment for exploring this difficult experiential dimension, a sensorium to complement other less vivid or less interactive media, a channel to experience, a route to inquiry that the students otherwise lack, with opportunity for interactive reflection. In particular, we aim to provoke and accomodate rich and perplexing emotional responses in the very process of ethical reasoning.

Pace the conventional wisdom that warns against emotional bias and fallacies, our emotions provide essential data for moral learnig. The difficult moral balancing act,the weighing and balancing of emotions and reasons together, can be learned only by doing. Interactive video provides a theater for practice and a safe ex-

ploratorium, for engaging emotions and reflecting criti-
cally on how emotions are informative, for addressing
one major challenge in moral education: finding ways
to accomodate, integrate, and balance both emotion
and reason, both powerful experience and careful reflection. But the medium of interactive video provides a
special kind of theater; it combines, in one technology,
the experiential *impact* of television or film, the power
of dramatic *visualization* to extend the moral imagination, with the freedom of movement and *control* afforded by the computer. The computer allows issues
that are vividly experienced to be carefully weighed re-
flectively explored.

Interactive video is a hybrid medium that can *complement* more traditional media to provide students a rich-
er experiential resource for extending their moral imagination and exploring their own and others' values. The
evident advantage of interactive video over other media
as a vehicle for delivering the stuff of vicarious experience is its *combination* of two crucial features of experiental learning: compelling *visual* experience – like
film, but unlike books – to extend the moral imagination where vivid first-hand experience is lacking; and
computer *interaction* to challenge the viewer and to afford the viewer control over the material, to enable reflection – like books, but unlike film.
*I try to bring the reader up close, so close that his em-
pathy puts him in the shoes of the characters. You hope
when he closes the book that his own character is influenced* William Carlos Wliams, in Coles,1987). The
videodisc is designed as a supplement to courses that
treat ethical issues, a sensotium for moral reflection

and inquiry. The objective is not to reach a body of theory or concepts, nor to chance users' ethical views, but to bring learners 'up close' to the human realities, moral perplexities, conflicted perspectives and sensibilities that confound our best efforts to chart and decent human lives. Whatever one's views in ethics, they require testing in the crucible of hard moral experience, experience often lacking in callow youth, experience that is not supplied in most classroom regimens.

The lessons taught by the videodisc, if lessons they be, are lessons in the imagination, sensibilities, and empathy required of component moral judgment and reasoning; lessons in one singularly necessary condition of ethical reasoning or theorizing: the vivid representation of the interest of others, the appreciation of the moral and practical straits that – but for the grace of fickle or our own feckless imagination – afflict us all, our common ground for negotiating conflict in community, without which we have only a community in conflict. A second objective, ironic as it may seem, is to bring users 'up close' to their very own (often inchoate and conflicted) values; to induce the self-knowledge and intimate reflection on one's own sensibilities so often neglected or impossible academic study, which suffers from what Robert Coles (1987) terms *the evr present temptation of the intellect to distance anything and everything from itself through endless generalizations* (one's own values included).

Dax Cowart's request to die poses the kind of hard choice and hard case that makes or breaks our theories about what is right, best or decent to do. Hard cases in ethics are born of rude realities, perplexing feelings, and conflicted viewpoints. But those rude realities rarely invade the groves of academe, while studied reflection is afforded amidst the presures of practical life. The videodisc aims to help bridge this gap between theory and practice, thought and feeling; to stimulate crucial conditions of moral reasoning in ways that other media cannot.

Competent moral reasoning requires more than ratiocination, *inter alia:* empathy, which presupposes the vivid representation of the interests of others; practiced confrontaton with hard facts, unforseen consequeces, and strong feelings; active deliberation under the duress of hard choices; an appeal, at once to our senses, sensibilities, and minds; with opportunity for challenge and reflection.

Exposure both to the affecting realities of 'real life' situations and the reflective opportunities afforded by academic study, the integration of emotional reaction and reflective reasoning about ethical issues, and the imaginative identification with the experiences and interests of others are the videodisc's basic objectives. We assume that the *integration* of emotional response and reflective analysis is a higher-order (more complex) skill than the dispassionate analysis of arguments and issues of ethical theory alone; and that, in 'real' as opposed to academic life, imaginative identification with others is presupposed by any competent rational reconstruction and critique of their arguments.

4 Impact: Lessons Learned

The content of the program is neither the theory nor

90

the concepts of ethics, but experiential data that any ethical theory or analysis must first behold in order to explain. The content is visual case material not delivered by ethics textbooks or other classroom media. The purpose of the program's content is not primarily to instruct, but to inform student' experience.

> Five decades of research suggest that there are no learning benefits to be gained from employing different media in instruction, regardless of their obviously attractive features or advertised superiority ... media are mere vehicles that deliver instrustion but do not influence student achievement any more than a truck that delivers our groceries causes changes in nutrition (Clark, 1983).

There is some ambiguity in the term *media*. If we grant this ambiguity, Richard Clark's notorius truck metaphor is useful for gainsaying or at least limiting his generalization, which (to be fair) applies to formal instruction in the formal content and methods of science and mathematics, We need to ask: What if certain groceries are not delivered at all? Nutrition will surely suffer. The aim of our videodisc is to deliver experiential content of a sort not deliverable by non-interactive media. For delivering vivid experience as well as reflective video is e vehicle without obvious alternatives.

I described above the *a priori* theory that informed design of this theater for ethical case study. Our first formative efforts to appraise the impact of the use of the videodisc by students ans medical professionals were limited to subjective questionnaires and debriefing.

During development in 1987-88, we field-tested the videodisc with over two dozen professional-level users (Dax Cowart himself, representatives of Concern for Dying in NYC, our psychiatric consultant, doctors, nurses, a ethics committee, media design experts, ethicist and other university faculty) as well as a small sample of students whom we observed and queried on their experience with the disc. In fall and spring terms of 1988-89 we deployed the revised pilot version of the program (0.9) with undergraduate students in two Carnegie Mellon ethics classes and with volunteer undergraduate nursing students at the Community College of Allegheny County (CCAC).

About 70% of our undergraduate users (who, by the way, were deliberately given no manual or briefing for use of the videodisc) objected to being required to give "Yes/No" answers to questions in the Guided Inquiries: the issues, they reminded us, are not black or white, but gray and fuzzy. These students did mot perceived the obviousness of this point to the developers or the intended heuristic value of said questions. This was a problem: a naive inquier should not be given any grounds for thinking the developers naive. We have subsequently changed this interface feature to a Likert-type scale in order to expressly allow shades of conviction and hypothesis as appropriate responses. To the other students and all of out professional-level reviewers the "Yes/No" mechanism was transparent as a heuristic for guiding their hypithesizing, for registering their inclinations. The epitome was a sophomore engineering student at a public demonstration who kept a large audienc engaged in animated controversy as he plied the pathways of the disc unencumbered by its mechanisms.

Apart from that feature, out initial audiences unanimously found the videodisc motivationally powerful and preferable to either narrative accounts or the linear video documentaries (which most had viewed beforehand), They found the disc to be more engaging, because self-paced, and more challenging, because of its combination of vivid confrontation and reflective opportinity. Few saw the point of the disc to be to change their minds or to argue any particular resolution to any dilemma; those who did only browsed the contents selectively. Most commented that they discovered a lot about their own dispositions and values and the they appreciated the opportunity to do so in private. Most remarked that the content made them less sure of what they believed, even if it did not change their mins; that the visual material showed the pregnancy and protean complexities of tha bare narrative 'facts' of the case. Most had very unsympathetic reactions to Dax's doctors (as they do with the documentary presentations), although this fact did not lead them to belittle the dilemma those doctors faced. Some students complained that the material was strong and hard to view.

This summary of users reactions is gleaned merely from the students responses to our questionnaires and conversation after the fact. One the while, these subjective reports and our own observations on the scene are in the ballpark of what we hope and expect, but ultimately they are just that, subjective reports, as arguably informative as the students' claims that my logic class has made them 'more ligical' or that our class discussions were extremely stimulating – which I'm often sure is in some important sense the case but endlessly questionable. One merit of the videodisc environment, which most users and reviewers have remarked, is that it provides a valuable new opportunity to query even research our own and others reactions to powerful material on difficult ethical issues in simulated 'real time'. But we have a long way to go to understanding its impact as well as the moral reasoning and learning processes upon which it purports to have positive impact. There is little evidence that anyone has developed or could develop ultimately clear objectives or success criteria in these *essentially contested* areas (cf. Gallie, 1968).

During these formative years, no attampt was made to compare the performance of videodisc users with non-users on any common assigned task of moral learning. But in 1989-90, Robert Kozma of the University of Michigan, while on sabbatical at Carnegie Mellon as a Dana Fellow in Educational Computing in the Humanities, collaborated with the author and Richard Young, a professor of retoric, on a formal evaluation project. Our subject were university students from Young's Argument & Controversy course and practicing professionals enrolled in the Medical Ethics Masters Program at the University of Pittsburgh. The goal of this study (whose published results are yet fortcoming at this writing) was to compare and document the impact of this medium with learning from 'informationally equivalent' presentations in two other media more frequently used in education, linear video and text. In particular, our objectives are to:

(1) describe the cognitive processes of students confronted with a complex moral task

(2) identify the relative impact of three media (interactive video, linear video, and text) on these processes and on learning outcomes

(3) examine the interaction between various individual student characteristics and these media as they affect cognitive processes and learning outcomes.

A comprehensive effort to evaluate the impact and educational utility of the videodisc will be long-term, if only because the modes of use (as a stand-alone resource or as a classroom presentational aid), possible audiences and settings (undergraduate ethics courses, writing courses, graduate or in-service professional courses), and allied tasks (for example, paper assignments, group role-playing as an ethics committee, specific tasks testing the congnitive and affective dimensions of moral learning) are so diverse. Another reason that assessment will be a long march is that there are several research agendas in terms of which to try to understand the videodisc's impact (for example, theories of ethical and cognitive development, gender differences in moral epistemology, moral controversy and the role of emotions therein). There is a good decade's work here. And we need follow-on efforts, a series of refinements as well as similar applications in ethics, as vehicles.

The intended audience for the videodisc is broadly postsecondary. We are collaterally testing the videodisc with two levels of audience: professionals (medical, university faculty) and undergraduate students. Our notion is hat the program and its content must pass muster in both undergraduate and professional education and the continuum between. The feasibility of this ambition is based on the assumption that visual media generally (film, TV) have a very wide 'bandwidth', the ability to communicate meaningfully albeit variously with audiences of diverse interests, maturity, and background. But, even if correct, this assumption does not obviate the need to be sensitive to designs that may serve one part of the audience spectrum better than another. For example, the videodisc does better, all things considered, with faculty and medical professionals than with undergraduate or (young) nursing students. One hypothesis is that the former are more mature methodologically, more able to balance competing hypotheses and conflicting intuitions when confronted with open-ended issues and confounding experience.

This points to one important dimension of future work: incorporating inquisitorial as well as navigational aids into the environment, heuristics that would illuminate the methodology of ethical inquiry. Our future efforts will expand on the current model of the videodisc as a moral sensorium and incorporate more explicit instruction in method and conceptual analysis. But the priority of this first foray into the interactive video medium for ethics is to emphasize *the primacy of experience,* to re-mediate and allow recovery from the abstraction of academic ethics. Merleau-Ponty's observation (1964) applies equally across the broad spectrum of our intended audience, in ehics as in other domains of human inquiry:

96

The idea of going straight to the essence of the thing is an inconsistent idea if one thinks about it. What is given is a route, an experience which gradually clarifies itself and proceeds by dialogue with itself and with others.

The Turn to Applied Ethics

Practical Consequences for the Role

of Ethicists in Public Debate

Introduction

What is the character of the contribution of ethics and ethicists in public debate? What are the limitations of this contribution? Which roles may the ethicist fulfill and which roles are less appropriate? An answer to these questions asks for a discussion about the nature of ethical 'expertise' and the character of ethical consultation. It also demands information and discussion about the development of ethical consultation in institutional settings, especially ethics committees.

In this section, special attention is payed to the French experiences with the functioning of a national committee on ethical affairs. Philippe Lucas, who is a prominent member of this committee, reports about his experiences, and describes the possible role of such an ethical committee in public debate, as well as the way in which this role is legitimized. But he also pays attention to the limits and the dangers of such a institutionalized panel of ethical reflection.

Although the national French committee on ethical affairs only has a purely consultative function, it is frequently made into a moral authority. This is partly due to the composition of the commitee: its members are representatives of various professions, civil offices, and religious or ideological traditions. The commitee may, therefore, acquire the (unsought) status of an 'ethical parlaiment'. But also the fact that the press writes about the commitee's proceedings as "prescriptions" contributes to the impression that the commitee is the primary national authority on moral issues. The behaviour of the press is not surprising, as ethical issues are 'hot topics' in France. Much of what used to be expected from 'politics' until quite recently, seems now to be expected from ethics.

One of the basic tasks of an institutionalized ethics commitee, therefore, is to make very clear that ethics is not something which can be dictated. Instead, ethics is something to be talked about by anyone. The committee only provides for themes, information and arguments for discussion. The question, then, is how a debate can be organized in a long-lasting way. Lucas notices that the number of occasions for public discussion seems to be decreasing.

As a first strategy in encouraging public discussion, the French national committee started to propose broad principles based on recommendations given at the end of court cases involving core ethical issues. These principles were amended and specified, while special ad hoc committees were asked to reflect on specific issues related to these principles e.g., respect of the human person, ethics and paediatrics, money and ethics and so on). In this way, the committee tried to show the public its involvement in a process of constant reflection, without making all its thoughts part of a closed doctrine.

The committee also decided to publish the divergent points of view of its members on certain issues, as it

102

realized that this divergence can only stimulate the public debate. Next to the organization of conferences and ethical discussions in the province (thereby trying to detect hidden forums for debate), the committee now pays special attention to setting up ethical training courses in higher education, and also at secondary schools.

The role and contrubtion of an institutionalized advisory board on ethical issues, therefore, is primarily educational. However, it seems unavoidable that its proceedings gain some authority. As Philippe Lucas remarks:

"In my opinion there should be a minimum of prescription, if only to avoid the disappointment of those who brought forward ethical problems. Also the committee cannot confine its proceedings to the defense and illustrations of "procedural" values, that is: democratic means." A minimum of moral authority, thus, not only seems unavoidable, but also indispensable.

The Role of the French National Committee on Ethical Affairs in the Public Debate.

Philippe Lucas

In France neither professional "ethicists" nor officially recognized ethical specialists exist. The members of the national consultative committee on ethical affairs, which was created in 1983 by a decree of the president of the republic, constitute no exception to this fact. The committee is a permanent organ; some of its members are replaced every two years. Most of its members are top civil servants or ordinary citizens. Before the creation of the committee, in the seventies, there were local ethical committees. Often these committees had been formed spontaneously in medical or university centres. Usually their aim was to give their opinion on research protocols. They soon became part of a rather important movement from which originated many militant moral groups – movements for the liberalisation of abortion and contraception, feminist movements, movements criticizing medical practices, and so on.

The national ethical committee's mission is to advise on ethical problems emanating from biological and medical research. In the light of this mission, the committee has got the task to organize annual conferences "on ethical problems raised by the humanities and the medical sciences". During these conferences there should be a public discussion of questions related to these problems.

The organisation of the anual conference does not seem to be too heavy an obligation; one should, nevertheless, realize that the work of the national committee is to a large extent guided and justified by its growing concern for the public debate. One could say that the public debate on ethical matters has actually preceded the activities of the committee, and that the committee more and more realizes that it has to serve this already existing debate.

I would like to focus on this evolution as it consists of a complete reversal of the committee's perspective. Taking this experience – better refered to as a test – with which the committee is confronted into account, I would like to describe the possible role of an ethical board in the public debate, as well as the way in which this role is legitimized and the limits which such a committee would have to face.

1. The committee's vocation to create and co-ordinate the public debate is much more the result of a trial than an intention. What trial am I refering to?

1.1 According to the foundation decree, the mission of the committee is of an advisory nature. The committe may be consulted by the parliamentary assemblies, the government, researchers or just ordinary citizens. Although the committee has a purely consultative function, it is frequently made into a moral authority or a magistrate because of its composition, and more importantly because of the questions it has raised and the way in which the press writes about its proceedings, often calling these proceedings "prescriptions". Moreover

106

judicial statements are to some extent based on advice of the committee. In other words, it seemed as if the committee's task consists of prescribing ethics.

Very soon, however, the public became aware of the fact that, in respect to its ethical authority, the committee does not differ from other magistrates, the state, churches, schools and professional communities: ethics is not something which can be dictated. Instead ethics has become something to be talked about, a theme for discussion.[1]

One of the most acute moments in this process of realization – and trial – which the committee had to go through, was the year 1984, when the committee, answering a request for advice on artificial insemination, asked the public authorities to organize "a far-reaching public consultation". It reckoned that "the debate on the interest of the future child and the right of its parents should be co-ordinated in such a way as to ensure a more open discussion in which all sectors of society should participate." Apart from setting up this public consultation, the committee would also "enable the french society to create the means and the time for necessary reflection."[2]

1.2 It is at this point that problems come up. How can the debate be organized in a long-lasting way?

The number of occasions for discussion seems to be decreasing. Only very rarely parliamentary initiatives come up in this field, while the French parliament has not held a substantial debate on ethical questions since the "loi vieille". The press seems to be imprisoned in a game of mirroring great events at the surface; more than the researchers themselves the press seems to be much more fond of grand medical premières than of open reflection. More important, the press continues to present the committee's advices as prescriptions that ought to be imposed without further discussion.

I am, by the way, not only refering to the "malice" of the press. Its readers and clients and French society in general "absorp" magistrates cases and decisions – and hence the committees cases and advices – even though these cases are not only powerful but also seriously ambiguous. In France there seems to be constant "ethical rumour".[3] What used to be expected from "politics" until quite recently, is now expected from ethics. There exists a large number of problems which were in former days considered to be social problems but are now treated as ethical problems. Many rights, which are often mere pseudo-rights, are suffering from inflation: the right to have a child, the right of a child to be born. These rights are now being refered to as embryo rights: the right to live, the right to give life, the right to receive life, the right to dipose of ones body and so forth. Having been stigmatized as absolute rights, one can only find them at the authorized depositories of petitioners, whose only function seems to consist of finding ways of justifying the magistrate's function, the magistrate himself hardly knowing what position he should take in this chaotic situation. Thus a very dangerous ethical exaggeration of the situation is being maintained.[4]

2. Considering the situation, how should one arrange the debate?

This is the problem the committee is confronted with. The committee has continuously tried to develop answers to this core problem, especially by thinking about a so called *educational dimension*. This dimension, it should be realized, was never part of the mission officially allocated to the committee.

2.1 The first "answer" of the committee has resulted from its methodological choice made just after its creation. Should the committee develop a doctrine right away and apply it according to the nature of the requests, or should it work in an empirical manner while taking into account the questions addressed to it? The committee has chosen a third procedure: It decided to propose broad principles based on recommendations given at the end of court cases. These principles would be amended and specified, while special ad hoc committees would be asked to spend time on reflection (thinking about ways of improving the respect of the human person, reflection on ethics and paediatrics, money and ethics and so on). In this way the committee could show to the public opinion its involvement in a constant process of reflection, without making all its thoughts part of a closed doctrine.

Apart from advising, the committee has developed the tradition of making two reports, namely a scientific report which focuses on scientific and technical development and an ethical report which aims at starting the public debate by reporting on te evolution of the committee's reflection, its presuppositions and viewpoints.

109

2.2 The development of the contents of the committee's advices and preoccupations is also of great importance. The committee is mainly concerned with economic problems (for instance the cost of diagnostic procedures) and questions related to health policy (such as prevention). The committee is no longer afraid of expressing divergent points of view – in particular on the problem of artifical insemination: it has realized that this divergence can only stimulate the public debate. Apart from organizing the annual conference, the committee has also decided to play an exemplary role by organizing ethical discussions in the province, discussing themes which do not necessarily have to be part of the committees preoccupations, by asking local ethical committees to provide the public with information and also by setting up an ethical training.[5]

2.3 In 1986, the committee decided to co-ordinate initiatives which aimed at setting up ethical trainig courses in higher education; it brought together universities which were interested in participating in courses, or had already set up trainings. As a result of these first experiences (in the medical sciences as well as in law and philosophy), certain training principles have been developed. It was decided that courses should be multi-disciplinary, that pluralism should be respected and that both practical experience and the public debate should not be neglected. In periodical meetings the committee has offered organisers for setting up some kind of control system as well as resource centres formed by the local ethical committees and the professional association. In the coming autumn the committee will organize together with these associations a training session.[6]

110

At the same time, the committee reflects upon a future ethical training in secondary schools, taking into account the "moral demand" of young people.[7] Quite often this demand is of an ambiguous nature. On the one side it cannot be separated from a latent fear which is sometimes manifest in the years before the youth's participation in "real" life, and is also present in a society which does not seem to know how to function properly. On the other side the moral demand is part of the so called school's "crisis", meaning that the school, following the example of the magistrates, experiences difficulty in "passing on moral values", or in other words: dictating ethics...[8]

Starting these ethical moral training courses involves the acceptance of the ambiguity I just described; the "crisis" and the problem of integrating new generations into society should be taken into account. Furthermore, these ethical courses logically imply that the real ethical debate should be led by young people, pupils and students, and older people at the same time.

3. Creating new opportunities.

As I have made clear, the committee is at present more concerned with the creation of new opportunities for discussion than with participation in traditional discussions which have already been part of the public debate for some time. This does not mean that the latter aspect is neglected by the committee: two years ago, for instance, we have organized a seminar on moral questions in the national assembly.

3.1 Even more important than bringing the debate back to life is the detection of hidden forums suitable for debate. This debate should neither only be related to the committee's activities nor to the ethical problems emanating from scientific and bio-medical progress. Professional or post graduate training may also, we hope, stimulate the debate in the future. Setting up these trainings should not just result in participation of the doctor and "his" patient in the debate. Hopefully, there will also be biologists who join in the debate, and other specialists in the complicated field of health care; why not also organdonors, blood-donors, administrators and other people who are concerned with the present developments?

Instead of talking about opportunities for public debate, one might also talk about the debating process[9] or debating procedures. One should try all direct ways to exchange information and intellectual products, having experienced the way of 'informing the public' by the militant moral movements in the seventies, and the efforts in the eighties to construct new information and communication techniques.

3.2 It is certainly difficult to measure the committee's influence in the public debate and the effectiveness of its approach. However, some indications do exist: First of al, the information networks surrounding the committee have caused it to revise its information policy. Secondly, the coming parliamentary debates will precede some law projects which are partly based on committee's advices. Thirdly, there is an increasing number of moral training courses; these courses are also attended by many members of the committee. The most important indication, however, is the change of atmosphere surrounding the committee's activities. This year, the committee will advise for the second time on the appropriateness of introducing obligatory AIDS detection tests. Undetered by strong demands, the committee has chosen not to propose authoritarian measures in this field. This choice, I may repeat, results from the committee's fear that the introduction of ethical measures would cause practitioners and their clients to loose their feeling of responsibility. Instead, the committee has proposed to develop and renew programmes aiming at information, persuasion and education. This proposal now seems to gain more and more acceptance.

3.3 Despite these positive indications, some problems remain. It remains unclear, for example, what the limits of the committee's role in the public debate are. Considering the present developments, one could even say that it has become more and more delicate to define these limits.

Even though it may not be as powerful as in other countries "ethical professionalism" definitely exists in France. Due to the committee's social recognition this movement has found more ways of legitimizing itself. Ethical "specialists" from several countries gather in international conferences in order to exchange information. There are, however, still people who neglect the positive development of the committee's activities and expect it to *prescribe* moral values. In my opinion there should be a minimum of prescription, if only to avoid the disappointment of those who brought forward ethical problems. Also the committee cannot confine its proceedings to the defense and illustrations of "procedural" values, that is: democratic means.

Finally, in reaction to these moral requests, and to the way ethics is used by the public at present (given the gross confusion existing among people), and also in reaction to the nearby elevation of the committee's members to a kind of saints, the committee has decided to become more and more careful in its proceedings.

Notes:

1. Lucas (Ph.), "Dire l'éthique" ("Dictating ethics"), Pris-Arles, Actes Sud et Inserm, 1990.

2. CCNE, "Avis sur les problèmes éthiques nés des techniques de reproduction artificielle"' (Advice on ethical problems resulting from artificial insemination techniques), Rapport, 15 décembre 1984.

3. Lucas (Ph.), "La rumeur éthique." Communication au colloque sur la drogue dans les sociétés démocratiues ("Ethical rumour", Symposium discussions on drugs in democratic societies), Association René-Descartes, Paris, 26-28 juin 1991, Published in "Drogues, politiques et sociétés", Pris, Le Monde éditions, 1992, p.71 sq..

4. Lucas (Ph.), "Les begaiements de l'éthique" (The hesitant beginnings of ethics), Revue des deux mondes, avril 1991, p.21 sq..

5. CCNE, "Avis relatif aux recherches sur les embryons humains in vitro et à leur utilistion à des fins scientifiques" (Advice with report to research on human embryos in vitro and their use for scientific purposes), rapport, 15 décembre 1986.

6. Lucas(Ph.), "L'éthique bio-médicale dans l'enseignement supérieur".

7. Sellier(M.), "Sciences du vivant, éthique et pédagogie", décem-

bre 1989.

8. Lucas (Ph.), "Enseigner l'éthique?" ("Teaching ethics?"), Lettre d'information du Comité national d'éthique, mars 1992.

9. cf. "Dire l'éthique", op.cit..

About the author:
Prof. dr. Philippe Lucas is Recteur de l'Académie de Bordeaux, Chancelier des Universités d'Aquitaine, and Membre du *Comite National d'Ethique Francais*.

Translated from the orginal French version (*Le Role du Comite National d'Ethique Francais Dans le Debat Public*) by Eric van Velzen, Utrecht.

About the Societas Ethica

The Societas Ethica is the European Society for Research in Ethics. The Societas has more than 200 members from approximately 19 countries, including both moral philosophers ánd moral theologians. The Societas Ethica is a platform for the exchange of scholarly work, ideas and experiences stemming from very different intellectual and philosophical traditions.

The Societas Ethica was founded in 1964. Since its beginning, it has strongly stimulated contacts between scholars in different countries, surpassing political, ideological and religious curtains. Both research in the analytical tradition and research in tradition of continental philosophy and theology has its esteemed place within the Societas Ethica.

Each year the Societas organizes a conference (mostly at the end of August). Members and non-members are invited to give a lecture or prepare a paper on the year-theme. The year-theme reflects an actual interest and debate in either applied ethics or fundamental ethics.

The Societas is bilingual: Engels and German are the official languages for conferences and publications. French is welcome, but cannot meet widespread understanding. Applicants for membership should be recommended by two sitting members and are invited to attend at least one yearly conference. Information about membership and conferences can be obtained at the secretariat.

Praesidium 1992-1994
(The praesidium changes every four years)
Prof. dr. Robert Heeger
Dr. Theo van Willigenburg
Dr. Wibren van der Burg

Secretariat 1992-1994
Center for Bioethics and Health Law
Utrecht University
Heidelberglaan 2
NL-3584 CS Utrecht

Fax: (NL) 30-533241